Anna School Learning

SUMMER MATH WORKBOOK

Step by Step Guide

Name:_____

Class:_____

Teacher:_____

Copyright © 2024-25 Anna School Learning
All rights reserved. This book or any portion thereof may not be reproduced or used in any manner whatsoever without the express written permission of the publisher except for the use of brief quotations in a book review.

Contents

Ratio, Proportion and Percentage	
Percentage	1
Percent Word Problems	5
Ratio and Proportion Word Problems	11
Convert Ratio, Fractions, Percent and Decimals	21
Algebra	
Order of Operations (PEMDAS)	24
Evaluate Expressions	27
Solving Inequalities	31
Verbal Algebra	36
Solving Equations (One Side)	40
Equations (Two Sides)	43
Cartesian Plane	
Cartesian Coordinates	48
Cartesian Coordinates (Four Quadrants)	51
Geometry	
Area and Perimeter	54
Pythagorean Theorem	64
Volume and Surface Area	70
Statistics	
Mean, Median, Mode and Range	80

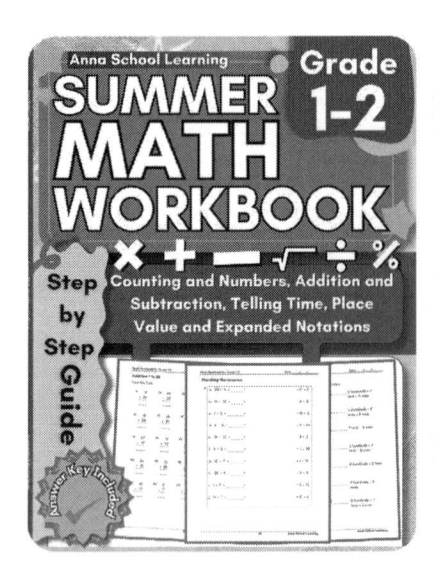

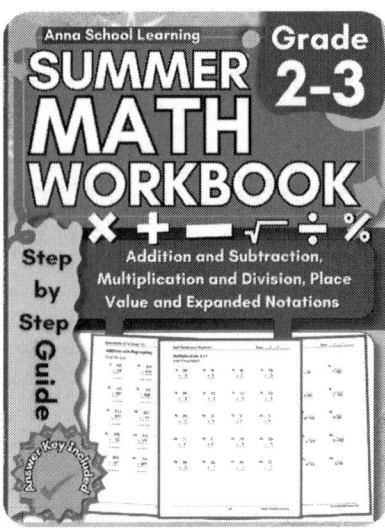

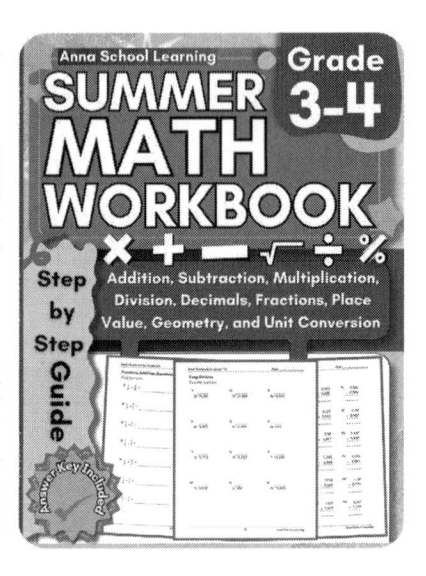

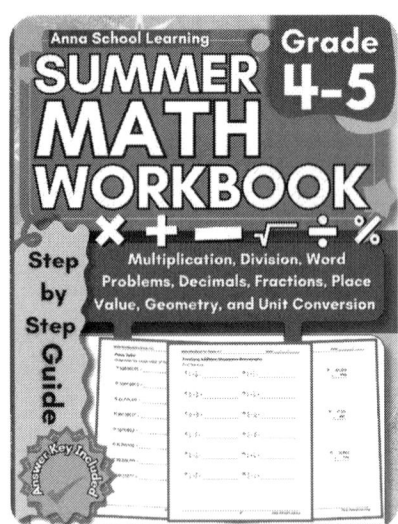

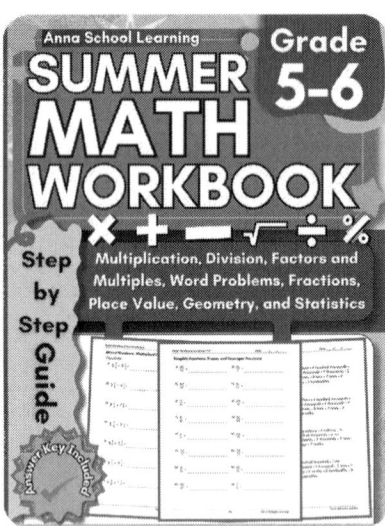

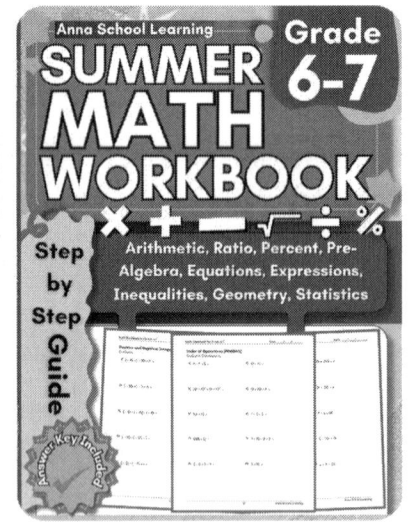

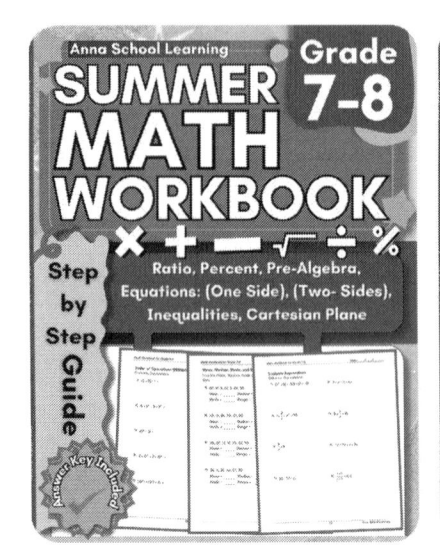

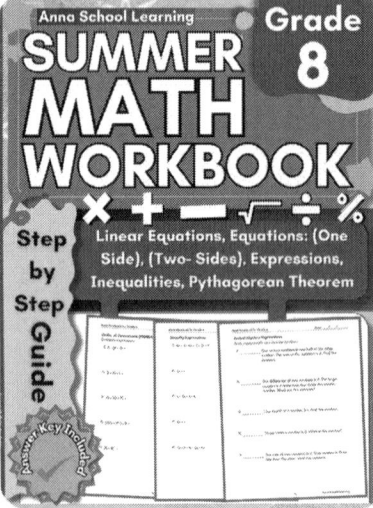

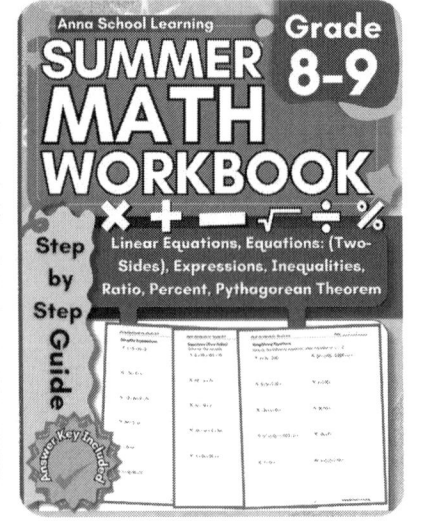

Anna School Learning — Summer Math Workbook Series

Grade 1-2
Counting and Numbers, Addition and Subtraction, Telling Time, Place Value and Expanded Notations
Step by Step Guide — Answer Key Included

Grade 2-3
Addition and Subtraction, Multiplication and Division, Place Value and Expanded Notations
Step by Step Guide — Answer Key Included

Grade 3-4
Addition, Subtraction, Multiplication, Division, Decimals, Fractions, Place Value, Geometry, and Unit Conversion
Step by Step Guide — Answer Key Included

Grade 4-5
Multiplication, Division, Word Problems, Decimals, Fractions, Place Value, Geometry, and Unit Conversion
Step by Step Guide — Answer Key Included

Grade 5-6
Multiplication, Division, Factors and Multiples, Word Problems, Fractions, Place Value, Geometry, and Statistics
Step by Step Guide — Answer Key Included

Grade 6-7
Arithmetic, Ratio, Percent, Pre-Algebra, Equations, Expressions, Inequalities, Geometry, Statistics
Step by Step Guide — Answer Key Included

Grade 7-8
Ratio, Percent, Pre-Algebra, Equations: (One Side), (Two-Sides), Inequalities, Cartesian Plane
Step by Step Guide — Answer Key Included

Grade 8
Linear Equations, Equations: (One Side), (Two-Sides), Expressions, Inequalities, Pythagorean Theorem
Step by Step Guide — Answer Key Included

Grade 8-9
Linear Equations, Equations: (Two-Sides), Expressions, Inequalities, Ratio, Percent, Pythagorean Theorem
Step by Step Guide — Answer Key Included

Percentage

Percentage is a way of expressing a number as a fraction of 100. It is commonly used to represent proportions, rates, and comparisons. The symbol "%" is used to denote percentages.

To calculate a percentage, we multiply the given number by the appropriate fraction or decimal equivalent.

How to calculate a percentage:

Convert Percentage to Decimal: If the percentage is given as a percentage value (e.g., 25%), convert it to its decimal equivalent by dividing by 100.

$$\text{For example, 25\% as a decimal is } \frac{25}{100} = 0.25$$

Multiply: Multiply the decimal equivalent of the percentage by the given number. This gives us the portion of the number that represents the percentage.

$$100 \times 0.25 = 25\%$$

Result: The result is the calculated percentage value.

For example, to calculate 25% of 80:

Convert 25% to a decimal: 25% = 0.25.

Multiply 0.25 by 80: 0.25 × 80 = 20. The result is 20.

Anna School Learning

Percent Word Problems

Percent word problems involve situations where percentages are used to calculate quantities or amounts. These problems often require converting percentages to decimals and then applying them to the given values.

For example:

Bella bought a pair of shoes for $90.00. If she paid an additional 90% for taxes, how much in total did she pay for the shoes?

- Bella bought a pair of shoes for $90.00.
- She paid an additional 90% for taxes.

Calculate 90% of $90:

Tax= 90% × 90

Tax= 0.90 × 90

Tax= $81

Add the tax amount to the original price:

Total cost= $90 + $81

Total cost= $171

Anna School Learning

Math Workbook for Grade 7-8   Date: ____/____/_____

Percentage
Find the percentage of given numbers.

1) 8% of 60 = ☐

2) 25% of ☐ = 150

3) 20% of ☐ = 120

4) 90% of 300 = ☐

5) 70% of ☐ = 350

6) 3% of ☐ = 12

7) 300% of 600 = ☐

8) 30% of 800 = ☐

9) ☐ of 900 = 45

10) 6% of 100 = ☐

11) ☐ of 800 = 16

12) 9% of 300 = ☐

13) ☐ of 600 = 210

14) 1% of ☐ = 1

Anna School Learning

Math Workbook for Grade 7-8   Date: ___/___/_____

15) [ ] of 200 = 160   16) [ ] of 500 = 375

17) 7% of 200 = [ ]   18) 4% of 700 = [ ]

19) [ ] of 900 = 90   20) [ ] of 200 = 400

21) [ ] of 800 = 800   22) 50% of [ ] = 300

23) [ ] of 600 = 90   24) 35% of [ ] = 35

25) 9% of [ ] = 0.9   26) 70% of 600 = [ ]

27) [ ] of 500 = 450   28) 4% of [ ] = 24

Anna School Learning

Math Workbook for Grade 7-8 Date: ___/___/___

29) [ ] of 500 = 250   30) 8% of 200 = [ ]

1) 49.8% of 68 = [ ]   2) 19.9% of [ ] = 184.672

3) 0.5% of [ ] = 0.03   4) [ ] of 733 = 164.192

5) 0.4% of 39 = [ ]   6) 0.7% of [ ] = 0.196

7) 0.4% of [ ] = 1.572   8) 17.5% of [ ] = 4.9

9) 29.1% of 434 = [ ]   10) [ ] of 420 = 30.24

Anna School Learning

Math Workbook for Grade 7-8   Date: ___/___/_____

11) [____] of 37 = 0.851   12) [____] of 1 = 0.367

13) 5.4% of 44 = [____]   14) 16.2% of 6 = [____]

15) 0.2% of [____] = 0.086   16) [____] of 52 = 5.616

17) 1.2% of 80 = [____]   18) [____] of 29 = 0.174

19) [____] of 6 = 0.024   20) [____] of 77 = 0.077

Math Workbook for Grade 7-8   Date: ____/____/_____

Word Problems: Percent

1) What is 5% of 80?

2) A school has a total of 78 teachers. If 50% of them are men, how many female teachers are there?

3) A classroom has 100 students, of which 5% are girls. How many boys are in the classroom?

4) Natalia bought a shoes for $96.00. If she paid an additional 25% for sales tax, how much in total did she pay for the shoes?

5) In a class of 42 students, 50% are boys. How many are boys?

6) A store has 20 apples. If 5% of them are sold at the end of the day, how many apples are sold?

7) Jason bought a bicycle that cost $70.00 when it was new. If he eventually sold it for 30% of the original cost, how much was it sold for?

8) A store offers 8% discount on all products. If the original price of scalpels was 25, what is the sales price?

9) Leah bought a camera for $56.00. If she paid an additional 50% for sales tax, how much in total did she pay for the camera?

10) A company wants to increase its revenue by 82%. If its current revenue is $50.00 million, what should be its new revenue?

11) A store offers 95% discount on all products. If the sale price of shampoos was 60, what was the original price?

12) A restaurant makes a pizza that is 84 inches in diameter. If they want to increase the size of the pizza by 50%, what will be the new diameter?

13) If the number 40 is decreased by 95%, what is the value of the new number?

14) A store increases the prices of all items by 25%. If the chocolates originally costs $8.00, what is the sale price?

15) In a survey of 58 people, 50% said they preferred android OS. How many people preferred android OS?

Math Workbook for Grade 7-8   Date: ____/____/_____

16) A teacher gave a math test with 8 questions. If a student got 50% questions correct, how many questions were correct?

17) Everly bought a bag for $72.00. If she paid an additional 25% for sales tax, how much in total did she pay for the bag?

18) In a school of 66 students, 50% of them take the bus to school. How many students take the bus?

19) Kinsley had a collection of 78 baseball cards. She gave away 50% of them. How many did she have left?

20) A school has 100 students. If 58% of them play football, how many students play football?

Anna School Learning

Math Workbook for Grade 7-8   Date: ____/____/_____

21) Serenity bought pens for $40.00. If she paid an additional 5% for sales tax, how much in total did she pay for the pens?

22) In a class of 4 students, 50% are girls. How many are girls?

23) Carson had 70 carrots. He gave away 30% of them. How many did he have left?

24) Ellie bought a book for $100.00. If she paid an additional 51% for sales tax, how much in total did she pay for the book?

25) A store is having a sale where everything is 50% off. The calendars originally priced at $8.00 is now on sale. How much is the new price of calendars now?

26) A person wants to make a 5% tip on a $60.00 meal. How much should the tip be?

27) A school has 50 students. If 58% of them play baseball, how many students play baseball?

28) In a basket of 8 globes, 50% are red globes. How many are red globes?

29) A store offers a 50% discount on all items. If Kaylee buys coins originally priced at $6.00, how much money did she save?

30) A car dealership sold 50 cars last month. If the sales increased by 8% this month, how many cars did they sell this month?

Ratio and Proportion Word Problems

1) If a recipe calls for three cups of sugar for every five cups of flour, how many cups of sugar are needed for 21 cups of flour?

2) A school has a ratio of four female teachers to every six male teachers. If there are 29 male teachers, how many female teachers are there?

3) A charity received a donation of $3,537 from a company. If the donation was divided among five charities in the ratio 2:3:4:5:6, how much did the fourth charity receive?

Math Workbook for Grade 7-8   Date: ___/___/____

4) A car travels 144 miles in five hours. How far can it travel in 10 hours?

5) A rectangular pool has an area of 398 square meters and a width of 16 meters. What is the length of the pool?

6) If eight workers can complete a job in 12 days, how many workers are needed to complete the job in six days?

Math Workbook for Grade 7-8   Date: ____/____/_____

7) If four workers can build a house in 12 hours, how many workers are needed to build the house in six hours?

8) In a bag of candies, the ratio of chocolate candies to fruit candies is three:six. If there are 14 fruit candies, how many chocolate candies are there?

9) A farmer has a ratio of two sheep to every eight cows in his pasture. If there are 47 cows in the pasture, how many sheep are there?

Math Workbook for Grade 7-8 — Date: ____/____/_____

10) A grocery store has a ratio of three apples to every nine oranges. If there are 48 oranges in the store, how many apples are there?

11) A company has a ratio of two managers for every 29 employees. If the company has 172 employees, how many managers are there?

12) A bus travels at a speed of 80 miles per hour. How long will it take to travel 200 miles?

Math Workbook for Grade 7-8 Date: ____/____/_____

13) A recipe calls for four cups of sugar for every five cups of flour. If you have 19 cups of flour, how much sugar is needed?

14) A train travels 182 miles in three hours. How far can it travel in 11 hours?

15) A school has a teacher-student ratio of 1:34. If there are 864 students, how many teachers are needed?

16) A company has a ratio of five female employees to every eight male employees. If there are 29 male employees, how many female employees are there?

17) A school has a ratio of five teachers for every 30 students. If the school has 155 students, how many teachers are there?

18) A charity received a donation of $3,345 from a company. If the donation was divided among five charities in the ratio 2:3:4:5:6, how much did the third charity receive?

Math Workbook for Grade 7-8 — Date: ____/____/_____

19) If a recipe calls for four eggs for every six cups of flour, how many eggs are needed for 11 cups of flour?

20) A charity received a donation of $2,304 from a company. If the donation was divided among five charities in the ratio 2:3:4:5:6, how much did the fifth charity receive?

21) If a recipe calls for three cups of water for every five cups of rice, how much water is needed for seven cups of rice?

Anna School Learning

Math Workbook for Grade 7-8   Date: ____/____/_____

22) A class has a ratio of two girls to every nine boys. If there are 29 boys, how many girls are there?

23) A bike travels at a speed of 11 miles per hour. How long will it take to travel 85 miles?

24) A machine can produce 190 units of a product in seven hours. How long will it take to produce 325 units?

Math Workbook for Grade 7-8 				Date: _____/_____/_____

25) If a recipe calls for four eggs for every seven cups of flour, how many eggs are needed for 20 cups of flour?

26) In a classroom, the ratio of boys to girls is three:seven. If there are 20 girls, how many boys are there?

27) If a map scale is 1 inch to four miles, how far apart are two cities that are four inches apart on the map?

Anna School Learning

Math Workbook for Grade 7-8 Date: ____/____/_____

28) Evan drives 234 miles in three hours. How far can he travel in 11 hours?

29) If a car travels 597 miles in four hours, how far can it travel in 10 hours?

30) If 10 chefs can bake 100 cakes in 17 hours, how many chefs are needed to bake the same number of cakes in five hours?

Math Workbook for Grade 7-8   Date: ____/____/_____

Ratio Conversions

1)

	Ratio	Fraction	Percent	Decimal
a.				0.158
b.				0.5
c.		6/11		
d.				1
e.		3/8		
f.				0.667
g.	6:7			
h.	5:7			
i.			71.4%	
j.			52.6%	
k.	1:13			
l.		2/7		
m.				0.941
n.	7:18			
o.	1:3			

21   Anna School Learning

Math Workbook for Grade 7-8   Date: ____/____/_____

2)

	Ratio	Fraction	Percent	Decimal
a.			75%	
b.				0.471
c.		3/5		
d.			84.2%	
e.	6:20			
f.		20/20		
g.			25%	
h.	2:5			
i.	6:11			
j.				0.467
k.		3/11		
l.	2:14			
m.	1:16			
n.		9/15		
o.				0.941

Anna School Learning

3)

	Ratio	Fraction	Percent	Decimal
a.	12:13			
b.				0.875
c.	10:14			
d.	8:11			
e.			35.3%	
f.			85%	
g.				0.947
h.				1
i.			5.9%	
j.				0.45
k.			94.4%	
l.				0.667
m.		1/2		
n.			25%	
o.				0.714

Order of Operations (PEMDAS)

The order of operations, often remembered by the acronym PEMDAS, stands for:

- **Parentheses**: Perform operations inside parentheses first.
- **Exponents**: Evaluate exponents (powers and roots) next.
- **Multiplication and Division**: Perform multiplication and division from left to right.
- **Addition and Subtraction**: Perform addition and subtraction from left to right.

The order of operations helps to clarify which operations should be performed first in a mathematical expression to ensure consistent and accurate results.

- **Parentheses**: Evaluate expressions within parentheses first. If there are nested parentheses, start with the innermost ones and work your way out.
    1. Example: $2 \times (3 + 4) = 2 \times 7 = 14$

- **Exponents**: Evaluate expressions with exponents (powers and roots) next.
    1. Example: $2^3 + 4 = 8 + 4 = 12$

- **Multiplication and Division**: Perform multiplication and division from left to right.
    1. Example: $2 \times 3 + 4 = 6 + 4 = 10$
    2. Example: $6 \div 2 \times 3 = 3 \times 3 = 9$

- **Addition and Subtraction**: Perform addition and subtraction from left to right.
    1. Example: $2 + 3 \times 4 = 2 + 12 = 14$
    2. Example: $10 - 4 \div 2 = 10 - 2 = 8$

Anna School Learning

Math Workbook for Grade 7-8   Date: ____/____/_____

Order of Operations (PEMDAS)
Evaluate Expressions.

1) $(5 + 7) \div 1 =$

2) $4 + 7 - 9 + 6 =$

3) $8 + 5^2 + 2 + 3^2 =$

4) $9 \times 5 \times 10 =$

5) $6(8 + 3) =$

6) $(4 + 7) \times (8 + 5) =$

7) $3 + 10^2 + 7 + 10^2 =$

8) $9 + 1 + 7 =$

9) $(10^2) \times (3^2) + 10 =$

10) $1 \times 5 \times 6 =$

Math Workbook for Grade 7-8 Date: ____/____/_____

11) $(4^2) \times (8^2) + 8 =$

12) $(10 \times 3) - (4 + 7) =$

13) $(10 + 6)^2 + (1 + 5)^2 =$

14) $(8 + 10)^2 + (1 + 2)^2 =$

15) $(8 + 10) \times (4 + 2) =$

16) $8 + 10^2 =$

17) $(3 + 8) \div 4 =$

18) $(10^2) \times (8^2) + 2 =$

19) $(2 \times 2) - (5 + 9) =$

20) $(7 + 8) \times (10 + 3) =$

Anna School Learning

Math Workbook for Grade 7-8 Date: ____/____/_____

21) $1 \times 4 + 2 =$

22) $(5^2) \times (8^2) + 9 =$

23) $2 + 3 + 9 =$

24) $(1 + 5) \times (3 + 3) =$

25) $(6^2) \times (9^2) + 7 =$

26) $(7 + 2) \div 10 =$

27) $(4 + 7) \times (5 + 6) =$

28) $8 + 3^2 + 4 + 9^2 =$

29) $3 + 4 - 1 + 5 =$

30) $(5 + 8)^2 + (8 + 4)^2 =$

Anna School Learning

Evaluate Expressions

Evaluating expressions involves substituting given values for variables in an expression and then performing the indicated operations to find the result.

For example: Let's evaluate $4x - 10$, when $x = 3$:

Step 1: Substitute the given value for the variable:

Replace every occurrence of x in the expression $4x - 10$ with the given value, which is 3:

$$= 4(3) - 10$$

Step 2: Perform the operations:

Perform the indicated operations according to the order of operations (PEMDAS - Parentheses, Exponents, Multiplication and Division, Addition and Subtraction):

$$= 4 \times 3 - 10$$

Step 3: Simplify:

Calculate the result:

$$12 - 10 = 2$$

Anna School Learning

Evaluate Expressions
Solve for the variable.

1) $(y^2 + 6) - 5(3 + y) = -13$

2) $5 = y - 2 + 6y$

3) $1 + \dfrac{8}{z} + 6^2 = 45$

4) $9 + \dfrac{z}{6} = 10$

5) $\dfrac{8}{x} = 8$

6) $72 = 9x + x + 2x$

7) $35 = 7(1 + z)$

8) $\dfrac{1+1}{y+4} = 0.4$

Math Workbook for Grade 7-8　　　　　　　　　　　　　　Date: ___/___/_____

9) $9 + (3z + 3) - 7 + (z) = 17$

10) $8 + \dfrac{1}{y} + 1^2 = 10$

11) $9 = \dfrac{y}{1}$

12) $6 = z(5 + z)$

13) $8x + x = 54$

14) $9(4x) = 36$

15) $7(4z - 4) + 5(1 + z) = 142$

16) $11 = (6x + 5) + (9x - 9)$

Anna School Learning

Math Workbook for Grade 7-8   Date: ____/____/_____

17) $4 = \dfrac{4}{z}$

18) $13 = x^2 + x - 7$

19) $z + 8 + 3z = 44$

20) $-27 = 9(6 - y)$

21) $8(2 + z) = 80$

22) $12 = 6z^2 + 6z^2$

23) $x(4 + x) = 5$

24) $(7z + 4) + (3z - 7) = 27$

Math Workbook for Grade 7-8 			Date: ____/____/_____

25) $(x)^2 = 25$

26) $\dfrac{9+4}{x+9} = 1.182$

27) $\dfrac{1+x}{x+8} = 0.222$

28) $6 = \dfrac{6}{z}$

29) $18 = 3(y)$

30) $33 = 5y + 3$

Solving Inequalities

Inequalities are mathematical expressions that compare the relative sizes of two values. They are used to express relationships where one quantity is:

- "<" (less than),
- ">" (greater than),
- "<=" (less than or equal to),
- ">=" (greater than or equal to),
- and "≠" (not equal to) another quantity.

For example:

$$y + -10 \leq -8$$

To isolate y, we need to get rid of the constant term −10. Since −10 is being subtracted from y, we can undo this operation by adding 10 to both sides of the inequality:

$$y - 10 + 10 \leq -8 + 10$$

$$y \leq 2$$

To check the solution:

$$2 - 10 \leq -8$$

$$-8 = -8$$

The inequality is true when $y = 2$

Anna School Learning

Math Workbook for Grade 7-8

Date: ___/___/_____

Solving Inequalities

1) $-8 \geq b + -10$

2) $\dfrac{m}{4} \geq -4$

3) $-6 \geq -5\,b$

4) $x - -9 < 5$

31   Anna School Learning

Math Workbook for Grade 7-8   Date: ___/___/____

5) $5 + y < 2$

6) $\dfrac{k}{2} \geq -3$

7) $8b > -4$

8) $9 > 6 - b$

Math Workbook for Grade 7-8 Date: ____/____/_____

9) $6 \geq -8 - y$

10) $3 \leq -3k$

11) $\dfrac{b}{2} > -2$

12) $-8 < 5 + z$

Math Workbook for Grade 7-8   Date: ____/____/_____

13) $-2 > 5 + z$

14) $-8 < \dfrac{k}{-6}$

15) $m - -4 \leq 2$

16) $8m \leq -8$

Math Workbook for Grade 7-8 Date: ____/____/_____

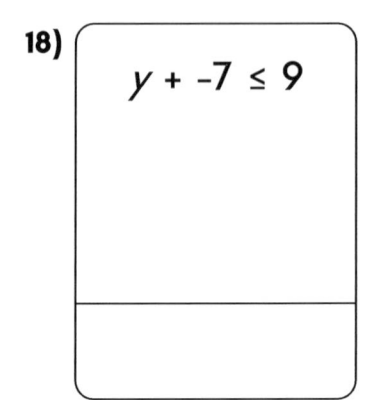

17) $-4b < 10$

18) $y + -7 \leq 9$

19) $m - 4 < 9$

20) $\dfrac{x}{-3} \geq 7$

Find Numbers (Verbal Algebra)

Verbal algebra involves translating word problems or verbal statements into algebraic expressions or equations.

For example: The product of the two numbers is 91. One number is six less than the other. What are the numbers?

We're given a verbal description of a problem, and we need to represent it using algebraic symbols and equations.

Let's break down the given problem into algebraic expressions:

- Given that the product of the two numbers is 91, we can write the equation: $xy = 91$
- Also, given that one number is six less than the other, we can write another equation: $x = y - 6$

Now, we can use algebraic techniques to solve the system of equations to find the values of x and y, which represent the two numbers.

$$x(x - 6) = 91$$

1. Solve the equation:
   - Expand the equation:
   $$x^2 - 6x = 91$$
   - Rearrange the equation into standard quadratic form:
   $$x^2 - 6x - 91 = 0$$
   - Factor the quadratic equation:
   $$(x - 13)(x + 7) = 0$$

2. Find the solutions for x:
   - From the factored form, we have two possible values for x:
   $$x = 13 \text{ or } x = -7$$

Anna School Learning

3. **Check the validity of the solutions:**
   - Since one number is six less than the other, we discard the negative solution.
   - Therefore, the solution is $x = 13$.

4. **Find the other number:**
   - Substitute $x = 13$ into the expression for the other number:

   Other number $= x - 6 = 13 - 6 = 7$

So, the two numbers are 13 and 7.

Verbal Algebra

Think Algebraically and find the numbers.

1) The sum of three consecutive numbers is 30. What are the numbers?

2) Nine more than a number is 15. What is the number?

3) The product of nine and some number is equal to the sum of that number and 32. What is the number?

4) The difference of two numbers is 31. The larger number is 7 more than five times the smaller number. What are the numbers?

5) If the product of six and a number is increased by 9, the result is 63. Find the number?

Math Workbook for Grade 7-8   Date: ____/____/_____

6) Nine less than a number is 9. Find the number.

7) The quotient of a number and six is 8. Find the number.

8) The sum of three consecutive even numbers is 18. What are the numbers?

9) Find two consecutive odd integers such that seven times the larger decreased by the smaller is 68.

10) The sum of a number and six is 15. Find the number.

11) Three more than three times a number is 15. What is the number?

12) Five times the difference of 15 minus a number is 45. What is the number?

13) The sum of two numbers is 30. The larger number is nine times the smaller number. What are the numbers?

14) The sum of four consecutive even numbers is 28. What are the numbers?

15) Three more than a number is 6. What is the number?

Math Workbook for Grade 7-8 Date: ____/____/_____

16) One number is three times another. Their sum is 20. Find the numbers.

17) Seven more than a number is 11. What is the number?

18) The product of four and some number is equal to the sum of that number and 27. What is the number?

19) The sum of the first and third of three consecutive numbers is 8. Find the numbers.

20) Two-fourths of a number increased by 2 is 10. What is the number?

Solving Equations (One Step)

Solving one-step equations involves performing a single operation to isolate the variable and find its value.

Let's solve an equation step by step: $16 + x = 31$

1. **Identify the Goal:**

    The goal is to isolate the variable x on one side of the equation.

2. **Simplify the Equation:** Combine like terms on both sides of the equation, if necessary.

    The equation is already simplified.

3. **Undo Addition or Subtraction:** If there's addition or subtraction involving the variable, undo it by performing the opposite operation on both sides of the equation.

    Since x is being added to 16, we'll undo this operation by subtracting 16 from both sides of the equation:
    $$16 + x - 16 = 31 - 16$$

4. **Isolate the Variable:** Ensure that the variable is alone on one side of the equation.

    $$X = 15$$

5. **Check Your Solution:** Substitute the value of x back into the original equation to verify that it satisfies the equation.

    $$16 + 15 = 31$$
    $$31 = 31$$

    The equation is balanced, so the solution.

Anna School Learning

Math Workbook for Grade 7-8 Date: ___/___/_____

Solving Equations: (One Side)

1) $10y + 3 = 63$

2) $11y - 20 = 2$

3) $m \div 14 = 3$

4) $36 - 3m = 3$

5) $y \times 5 = 60$

6) $k + 9 = 15$

7) $8 - m = 2$

8) $11 = 14 - k$

9) $m \div 2 = 11$

10) $255 = k \times 17$

Math Workbook for Grade 7-8   Date: ____/____/_____

11) $11 + m = 25$

12) $22 \div y = 11$

13) $15 = 120 \div z$

14) $128 - 15k = 8$

15) $28 = 3m + 13$

16) $90 = z \times 15$

17) $k \div 14 = 9$

18) $280 \div y = 14$

19) $12 = 2 \times k$

20) $15m + 14 = 119$

Anna School Learning

Math Workbook for Grade 7-8   Date: ____/____/_____

21) k + 10 = 30

22) 72 = 6 × z

23) 258 = 6 + 14z

24) 6 + 19k = 196

25) 9 + k = 25

26) 11m + 7 = 29

27) 6 = 18 - 1y

28) 0 = 45 - 15z

29) 13 = x + 3

30) 45 ÷ z = 5

Equations (Two Sides)

A two-sided equation is an equation where both sides have expressions with variables and constants. The goal when solving a two-sided equation is to find the value of the variable that makes both sides equal.

For example: Let's solve an equation:

$$9 + 8x + 8 = 64 + x + 2$$

- **Combine Like Terms:** Simplify each side of the equation by combining like terms (terms with the same variable or constants).

  $$9 + 8x + 8 = 64 + x + 2$$
  $$17 + 8x = 66 + x$$

- **Isolate the Variable:** Use inverse operations to isolate the variable on one side of the equation.

  subtract x from both sides:

  $$17 + 8x - x = 66 + x - x$$
  $$17 + 7x = 66$$

  subtracting 17 from both sides:

  $$17 - 17 + 7x = 66 - 17$$
  $$7x = 49$$

  divide both sides by 7:

  $$\frac{7x}{7} = \frac{49}{7} = x = 7$$

- **Check Solution:** Once you find the solution, substitute it back into the original equation to ensure it makes the equation true.

  Substitute $x = 7$ back into the original equation:

  $$9 + 8(7) + 8 = 64 + 7 + 2$$
  $$9 + 56 + 8 = 64 + 7 + 2$$
  $$73 = 73$$

Anna School Learning

Math Workbook for Grade 7-8   Date: ____/____/_____

Equations (Two Sides)
Solve for the variable.

1) $9 + 8y = 72 + y$

2) $9 + 7y = 45 + y$

3) $8 + m = 3m$

4) $1 + 5z = 11 + 3z$

5) $2k = 3 + k$

6) $5x + 3 = 15 + x$

7) $19 + y + -1 = 9 + 5y + 1$

8) $72 - z = 4 + 6z + 5$

9) $9 + 8m + 6 = 33 - m$

10) $10 + 8m = 9m + 1$

11) $1 + 2m = 8 + m$

12) $4 + 7k + 9 = 16 + k + 3$

13) $61 + m = 7 + 7m$

14) $3 + 5y = 9 - y$

15) $6 + 8x + 9 = 62 + x + 2$

16) $40 + x = 8 + 6x + 7$

17) $9k + 8 = 96 - 2k$

Math Workbook for Grade 7-8   Date: ____/____/_____

18) $3x = 16 + x$

19) $32 - x = 8 + 8x + 6$

20) $6z = 28 - z$

21) $16 + x = 2x + 9$

22) $17 - m = 1 + 3m$

23) $31 + x = 5x + 3$

Math Workbook for Grade 7-8　　　　　　　　　　　　　　　　　Date: ____/____/_____

24) $44 - y = 2 + 5y$

25) $3 + 8z + 5 = 53 - z$

26) $30 + y = 6y$

27) $9 + 6z + 8 = 42 + z$

28) $5 + k = 6k$

29) $36 - z + 12 = 8 + 8z + 4$

Cartesian Coordinates

The Cartesian Coordinate System, also known as the x-y plane, provides a method for representing points on a graph using two perpendicular lines: the x-axis and the y-axis. At their intersection, denoted by the letter "O", lies the origin.

To plot a point on this system, we use coordinates, consisting of two numbers. The first number represents the horizontal movement from the origin (x-coordinate), while the second number represents the vertical movement (y-coordinate). These coordinates are written as an ordered pair (x, y).

For instance, let's plot these coordinates:

$A = (1, 3)$ $B = (5, 0)$ $C = (8, 6)$

$D = (9, 5)$ $E = (1, 9)$ $F = (3, 1)$

$G = (0, 8)$ $H = (4, 6)$ $I = (4, 9)$

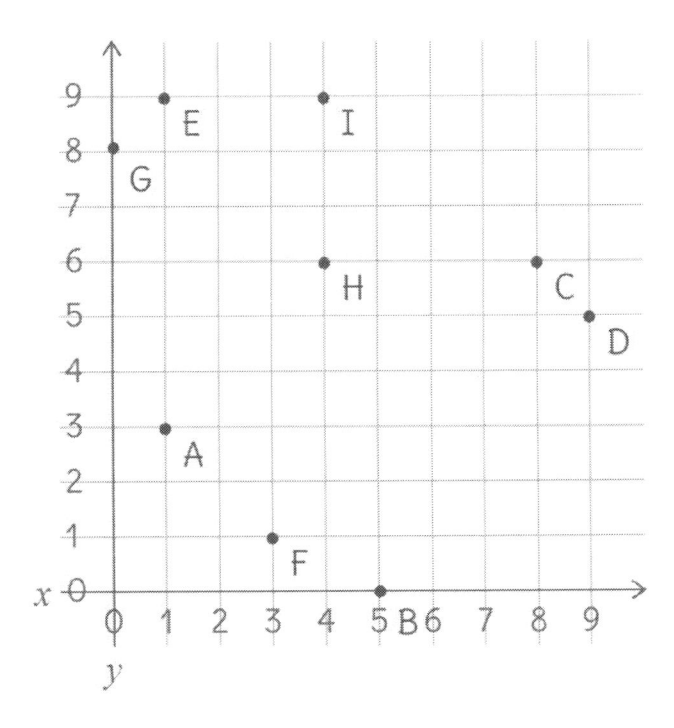

Anna School Learning

Cartesian Coordinates (Four Quadrants)

In a Cartesian coordinate system with four quadrants, there are two perpendicular number lines intersecting at the origin (0,0), dividing the plane into four quadrants.

To plot a point in this Cartesian coordinate system, we use an ordered pair (x, y), where x represents the distance from the y-axis, and y represents the distance from the x-axis.

For instance, let's plot these coordinates:

A = (-4, 1)   B = (2, 1)   C = (4, 2)

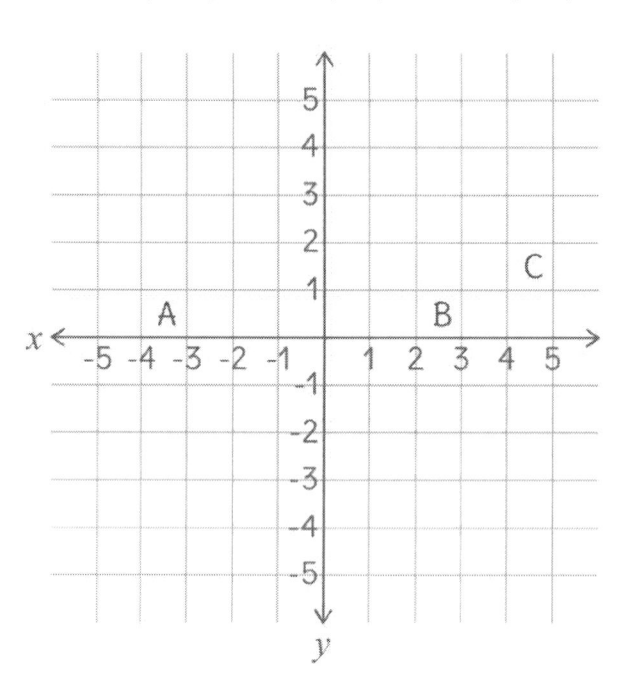

Anna School Learning

Cartesian Coordinates
Fill in as indicated.

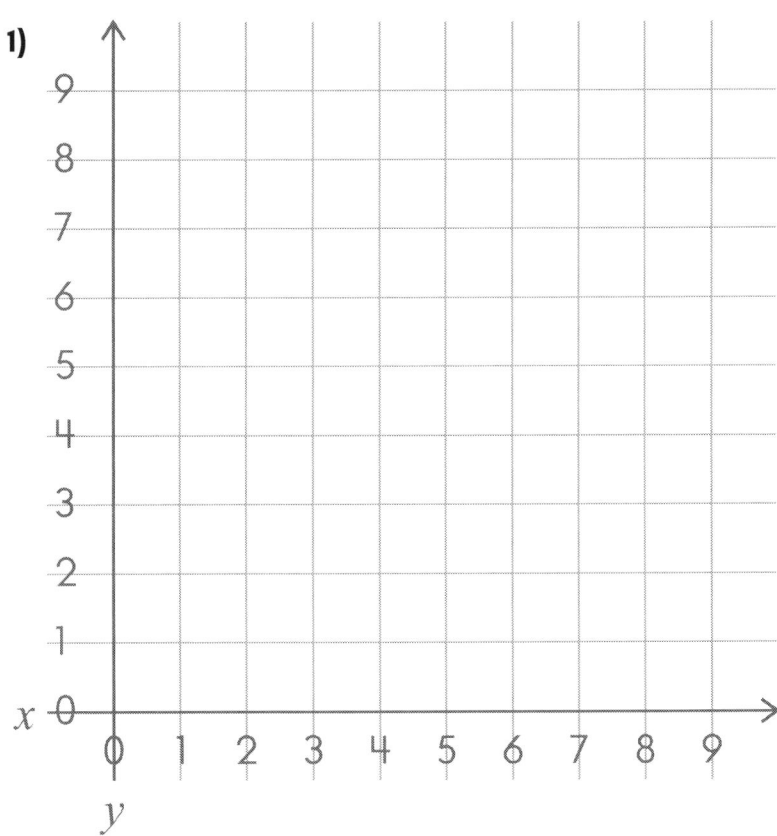

1)

A = (5, 2)   B = (6, 2)   C = (4, 9)

D = (9, 6)   E = (6, 8)   F = (3, 8)

G = (8, 7)   H = (8, 4)   I = (5, 7)

Math Workbook for Grade 7-8 Date: ____/____/_____

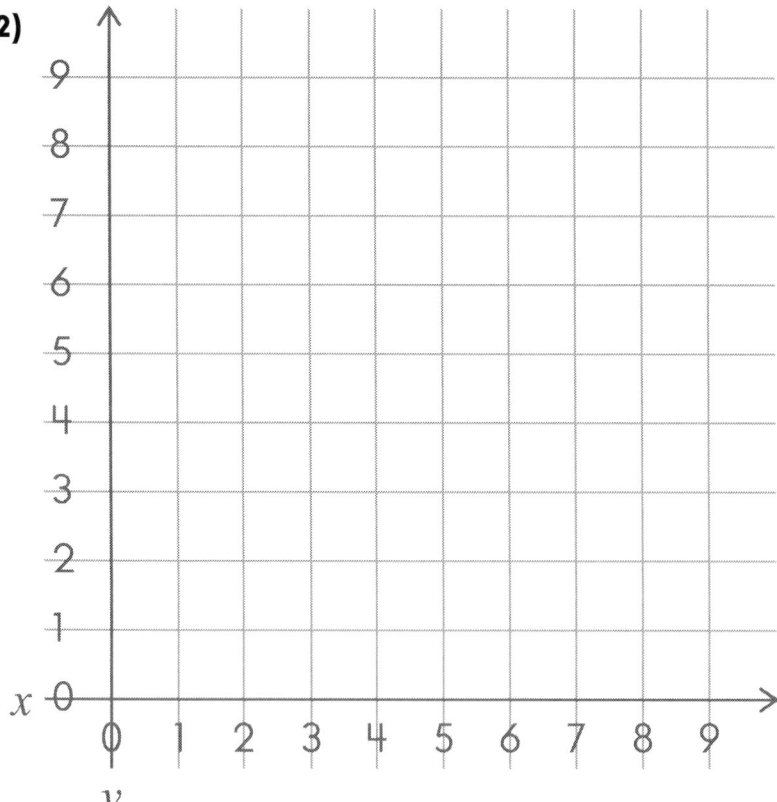

2)

A = (0, 6)   B = (0, 2)   C = (2, 8)

D = (9, 1)   E = (3, 1)   F = (7, 0)

G = (4, 6)   H = (5, 9)   I = (6, 0)

Math Workbook for Grade 7-8 Date: ____/____/_____

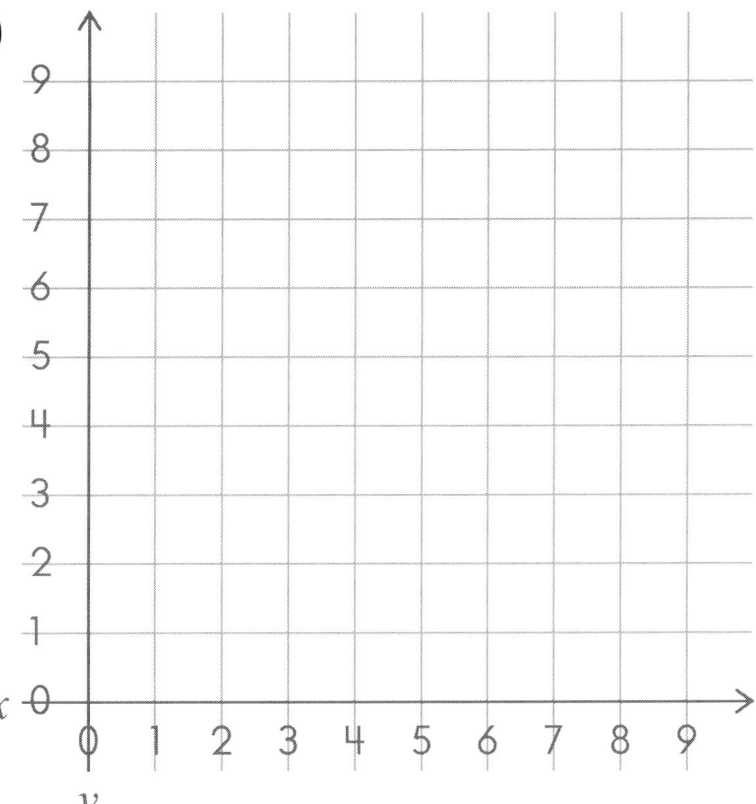

3)

A = (7, 8)   B = (8, 7)   C = (5, 9)

D = (4, 6)   E = (0, 1)   F = (6, 5)

G = (7, 1)   H = (3, 8)   I = (8, 5)

Cartesian Coordinates With Four Quadrants

Fill in as indicated.

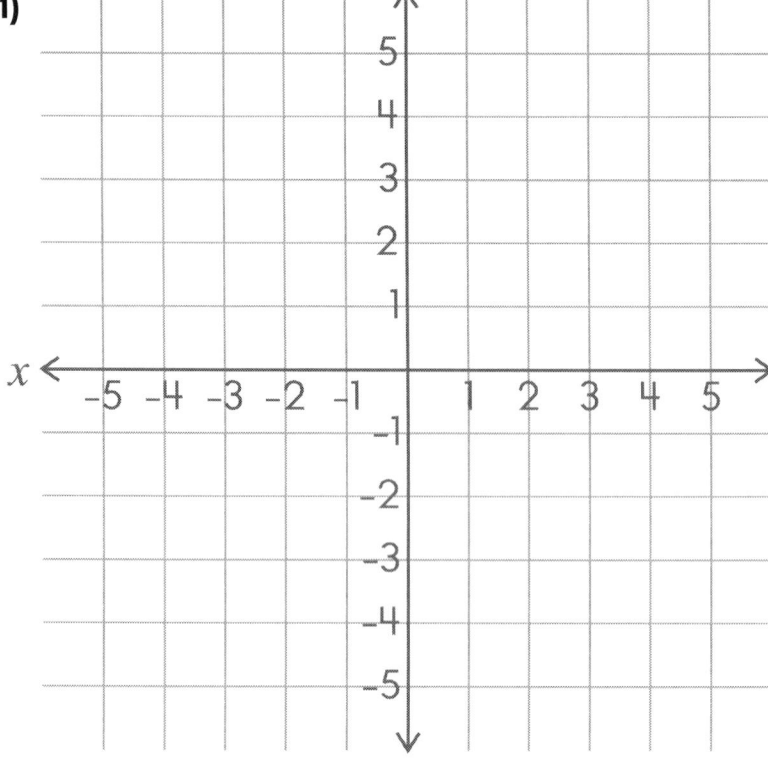

1)

A = (3, −2)   B = (−5, 3)   C = (−3, −2)

D = (1, 4)   E = (4, 2)   F = (0, 3)

G = (−3, 4)   H = (−4, 3)   I = (3, 1)

Math Workbook for Grade 7-8　　　　　　　　　　　　　　Date: ____/____/_____

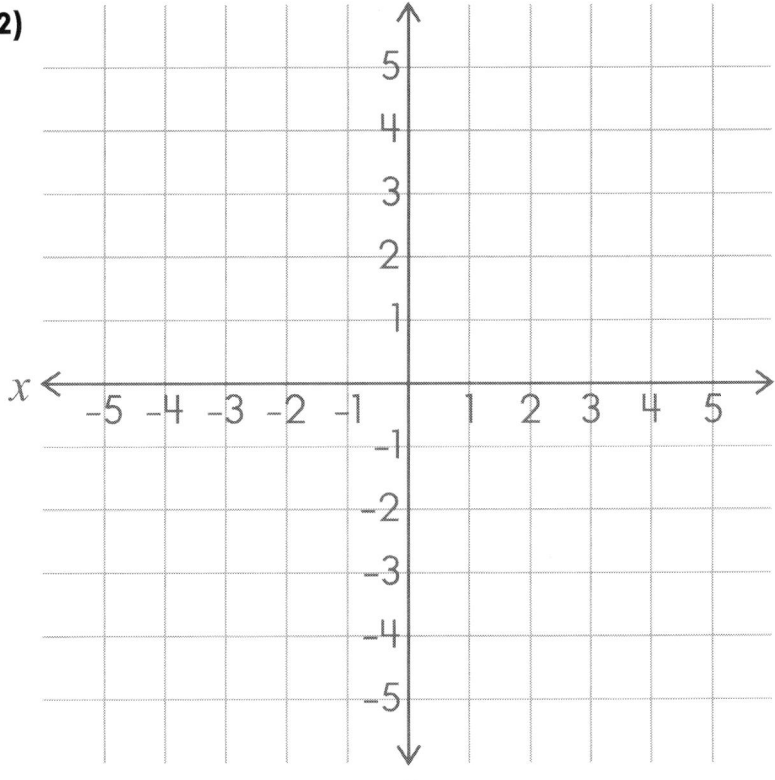

2)

A = (5, -2)　　B = (-5, -3)　　C = (3, 1)

D = (3, 4)　　E = (0, 4)　　F = (-1, 1)

G = (2, 1)　　H = (4, -5)　　I = (-3, -2)

Math Workbook for Grade 7-8   Date: ____/____/_____

3)

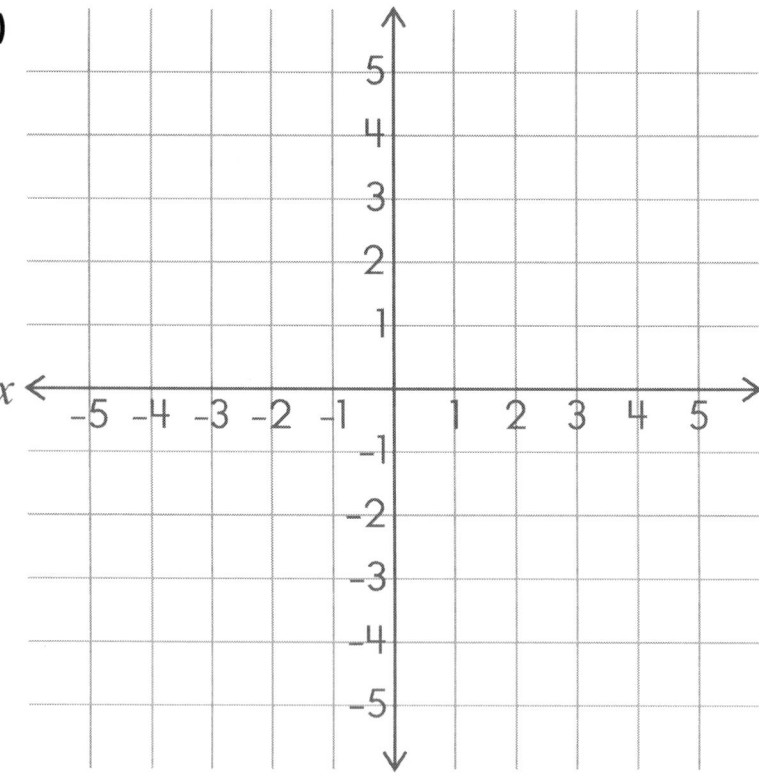

A = (-5, -5)   B = (2, 0)   C = (-4, 3)

D = (5, 3)   E = (-3, -2)   F = (4, 4)

G = (-1, 5)   H = (-1, 2)   I = (5, 0)

Area and Perimeter

The area of a shape represents the amount of space it occupies. The perimeter of a shape is the total distance around its outer edge.

Area of Rectangle

For a square, since all four sides are equal, we only need to know the length of one side to find its area. We can calculate the area of a square by multiplying the length of one side by itself (squared). So, if the length of one side of the square is 's', then the area (A) is given by:

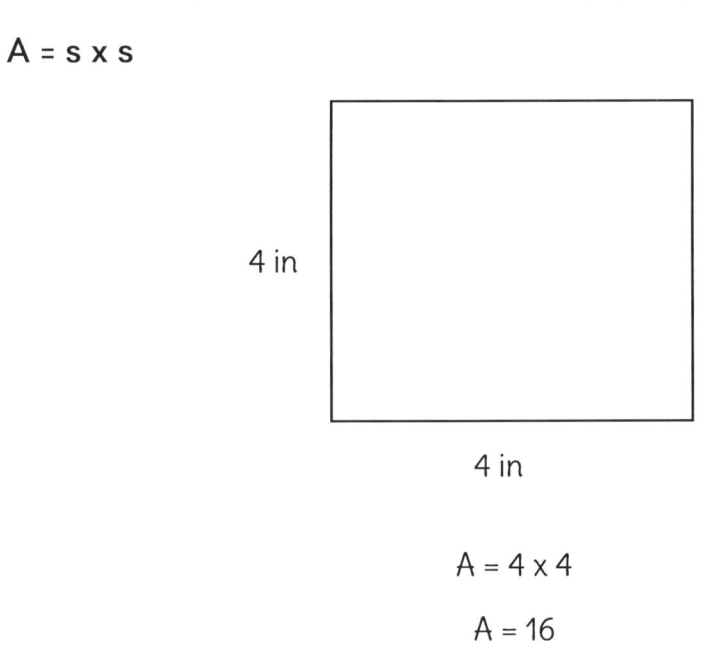

A = s x s

4 in

4 in

A = 4 x 4

A = 16

Anna School Learning

Perimeter of Rectangle

For a square, since all four sides are equal, we can find the perimeter by adding up the lengths of all four sides. If 's' represents the length of one side, then the perimeter (P) is given by:

$$P = 4 \times s$$
$$P = 4 \times 4$$
$$P = 16$$

Area of Triangle:

The area of a triangle represents the amount of space enclosed within its three sides. The formula for calculating the area of a triangle depends on the type of triangle. For a general triangle, we use the formula:

$$A = \frac{1}{2} \times base \times height$$

Where:

- A represents the area of the triangle.
- The base is the length of any one side of the triangle.
- The height is the perpendicular distance from the base to the opposite vertex.

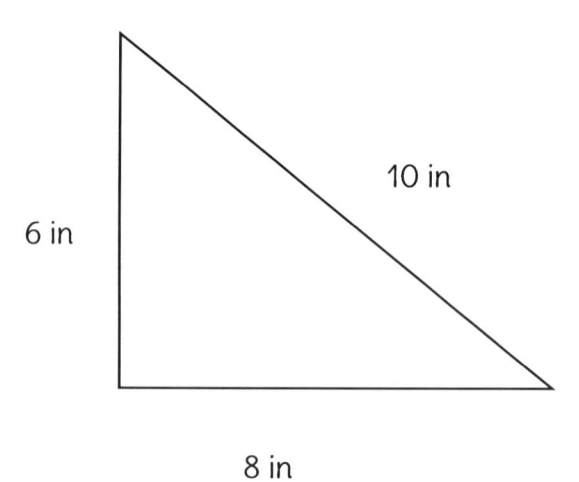

6 in

10 in

8 in

Anna School Learning

$$A = \frac{1}{2} \times \text{base} \times \text{height}$$

$$A = \frac{1}{2} \times 6 \times 8$$

$$A = \frac{1}{2} \times 48$$

$$A = 24$$

Perimeter of Triangle:

The perimeter of a triangle is the total length of its three sides. To find the perimeter, we simply add the lengths of all three sides together:

$$P = side1 + side2 + side3$$

$$P = 6 + 8 + 10$$

$$P = 24$$

Equilateral Triangle

An equilateral triangle is a triangle in which all three sides are equal in length. To find the area and perimeter of an equilateral triangle, we can use the following formulas:

- Area (A): $\frac{\sqrt{3}}{4} \times a^2$ where a is the length of one side of the equilateral triangle.
- Perimeter (P): $P = 3a$ where a is the length of one side of the equilateral triangle.

Let's solve a problem:

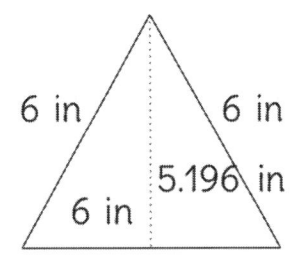

6 in / 6 in
5.196 in
6 in

Anna School Learning

Area of Equilateral Triangle:

$$\text{Area (A)}: \frac{\sqrt{3}}{4} \times (6)^2$$

$$\text{Area (A)}: \frac{\sqrt{3}}{4} \times 36$$

$$\text{Area (A)}: \frac{36\sqrt{3}}{4}$$

$$\text{Area (A)}: \frac{36(1.73)}{4}$$

$$\text{Area (A)}: \frac{62.35}{4}$$

$$\text{Area (A)}: 15.59 \text{ in}^2$$

Perimeter of Equilateral Triangle:

$$P = 3a$$

$$P = 3(6) = 18$$

Isosceles Triangle

An isosceles triangle is a triangle with at least two sides of equal length. The angles opposite the equal sides are also equal.

Area of Isosceles Triangle

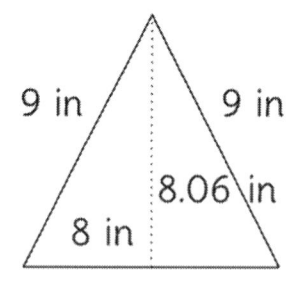

$$A = \frac{1}{2} \times \text{base} \times \text{height}$$

$$A = \frac{1}{2} \times 8 \times 8$$

Anna School Learning

$$A = \frac{1}{2} \times 64$$

$$A = 32$$

Perimeter of Isosceles Triangle

The perimeter of a triangle is the total length of its three sides. To find the perimeter, we simply add the lengths of all three sides together:

$$P = side1 + side2 + side3$$

$$P = 9 + 9 + 8$$

$$P = 26$$

Scalene Triangle

A scalene triangle is a triangle with no equal sides and no equal angles. The formula for finding various properties of a scalene triangle is as follows:

Area (A): The area of a scalene triangle can be calculated using Heron's formula, which is given by:

$$A = \sqrt{s(s-a)(s-b)(s-c)}$$

where *s* is the semi-perimeter of the triangle,

and *a*, *b*, and *c* are the lengths of its three sides.

Perimeter (P): The perimeter of a scalene triangle is the sum of the lengths of its three sides.

$$P = side1 + side2 + side3$$

Anna School Learning

Let's find the Area and Perimeter of a Scalene Triangle:

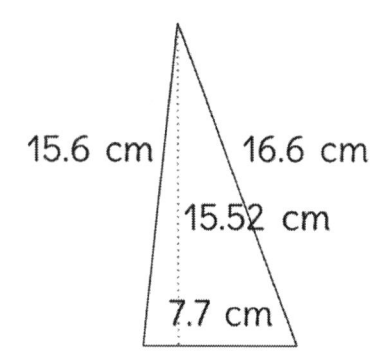

15.6 cm   16.6 cm
15.52 cm
7.7 cm

Area (A): First, we calculate the semi-perimeter (*s*):

$$S = \frac{a+b+c}{2} = \frac{15.6 + 16.6 + 7.7}{2} = \frac{39.8}{2} = 19.9 \text{ cm}$$

Heron's formula to find the area:

$$A = \sqrt{s(s-a)(s-b)(s-c)}$$

$$A = \sqrt{19.9 \, (19.9 - 15.6)(19.9 - 16.6)(19.9 - 7.7)}$$

$$A = \sqrt{19.9 \times 4.3 \times 3.3 \times 12.2}$$

$$A = \sqrt{3445} \approx 59$$

Perimeter (P):

$$P = side1 + side2 + side3$$

$$P = 15.6 + 16.6 + 7.7$$

$$P = 39.8$$

Anna School Learning

Area and Perimeter of an L-shape

The L-shaped figure typically consists of two rectangles joined together to form an L-shape. To find the area and perimeter of an L-shaped figure, we will need to calculate the areas and perimeters of each rectangle and then combine them.

Area=Area of Rectangle 1 + Area of Rectangle 2

Perimeter=Perimeter of Rectangle 1 + Perimeter of Rectangle 2

Let's find the Area and Perimeter of an L-shape:

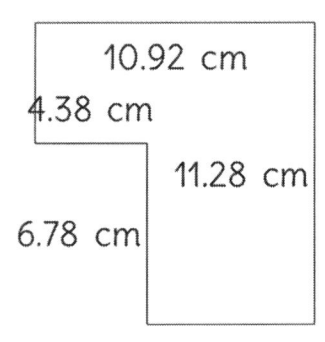

```
         10.92 cm
   4.38 cm
                  11.28 cm
   6.78 cm
```

Area of L-Shape

Area 1 = 4.38 x 4.5 = 19.7 cm^2

Area 2 = 11.28 x 6.54 = 73.7 cm^2

Area = 19.7 + 73.7

Area = 93.481 cm^2

Perimeter of L-Shape

P = 11.28 + 6.54 + 6.78 + 4.38 + 4.5 + 10.92

P = 44.4 cm

Anna School Learning

Area and Perimeter of U-shape

U-shape is basically composed of three rectangles, we'll need to calculate the area and perimeter of each rectangle separately and then sum them up.

Area of the U-shape:

The total area (A) of the U-shape is the sum of the areas of the three rectangles:

$$A = A1 + A2 + A3$$

Perimeter of the U-shape: The total perimeter (P) of the U-shape is the sum of the perimeters of the three rectangles:

$$P = P1 + P2 + P3$$

Let's find the area and perimeter of the following U-shape:

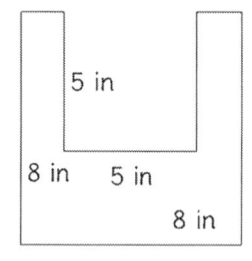

```
       5 in

  8 in    5 in
            8 in
```

Area:

$$A1 = 8 \times 1.5 = 12 + A2 = 3 \times 5 = 15 + A3 = 8 \times 1.5 = 12$$

$$= 12 + 15 + 12$$

$$= 39 \text{ in}^2$$

Perimeter:

$$2 \times 8 + 2 \times 5 + 2 \times 8$$

$$= 16 + 10 + 16$$

$$= 42$$

Anna School Learning

Math Workbook for Grade 7-8 Date: ___/___/_____

Area and Perimeter

1)
- 10 in
- 5 in
- 11 in
- 6 in

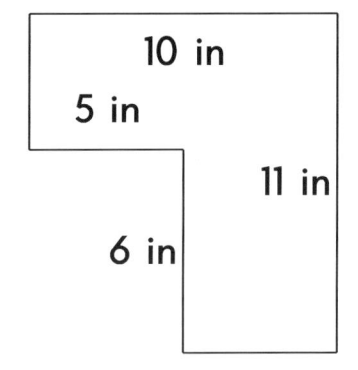

2)
- 17 in
- 17 in
- 15.49 in
- 14 in

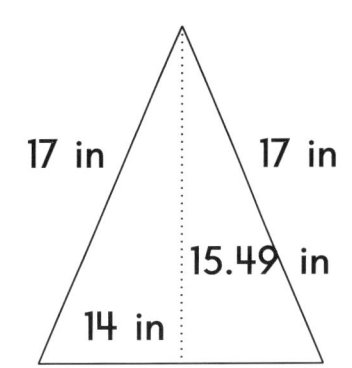

3)
- 20 in
- 12 in
- 16 in

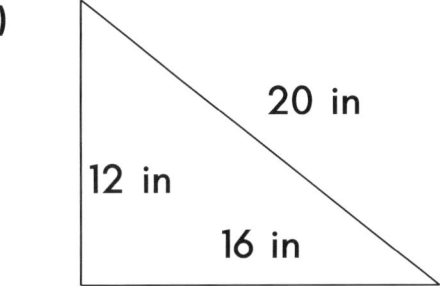

4)
- 13 in
- 13 in
- 14 in

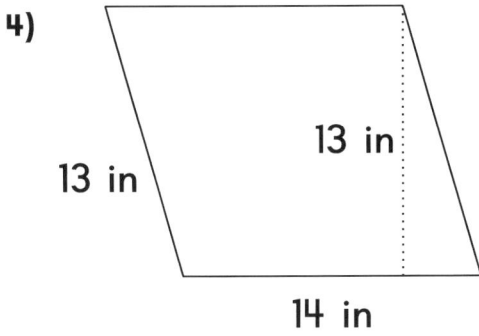

Math Workbook for Grade 7-8   Date: ____/____/_____

5)
14 in 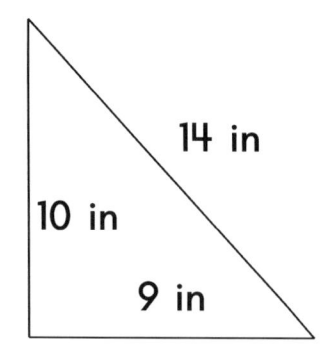
10 in
9 in

6)
13 in 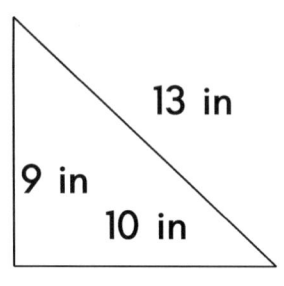
9 in
10 in

7)
11 in   11 in 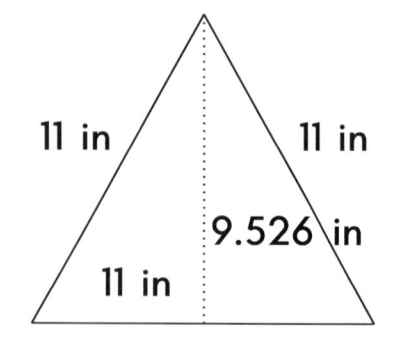
9.526 in
11 in

8)
10 in 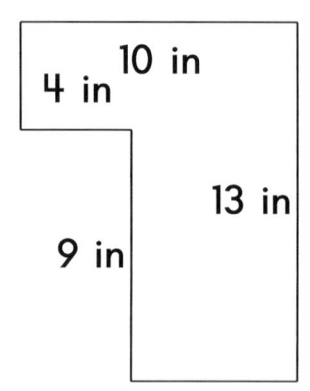
4 in
13 in
9 in

Math Workbook for Grade 7-8   Date: ____/____/_____

9)

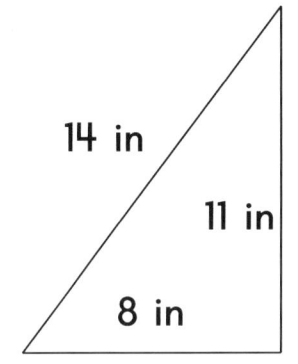

14 in
11 in
8 in

10)

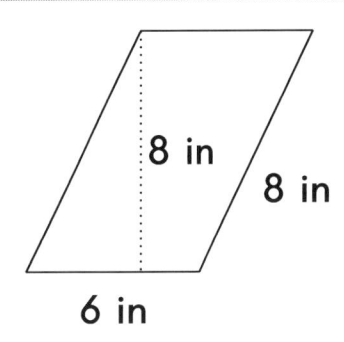

8 in
8 in
6 in

11)

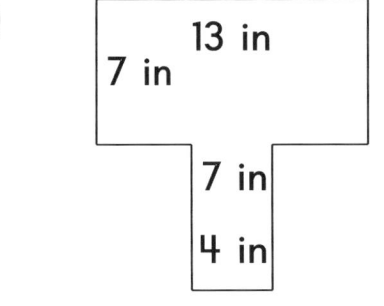

13 in
7 in
7 in
4 in

12)

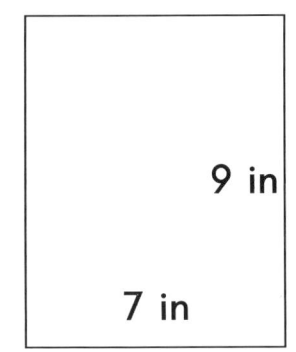

9 in
7 in

Math Workbook for Grade 7-8   Date: ___/___/____

13)

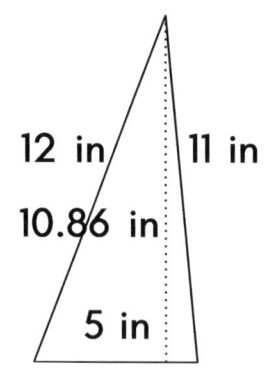

12 in   11 in
10.86 in
5 in

14)

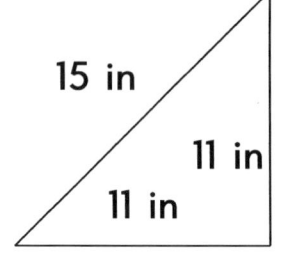

15 in
11 in
11 in

15)

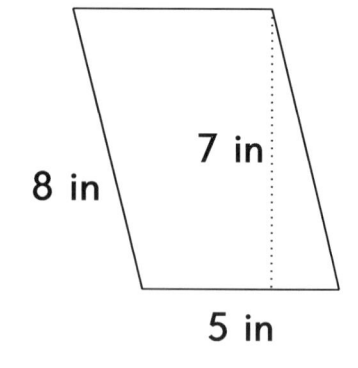

8 in
7 in
5 in

16)

10 in
7 in
7 in

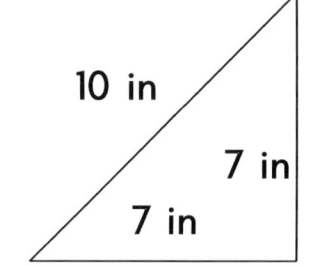

Math Workbook for Grade 7-8   Date: ____/____/_____

17)

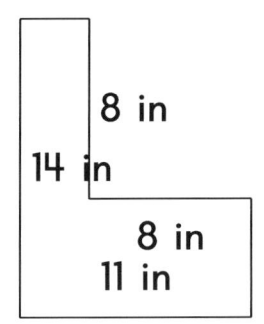

8 in
14 in
8 in
11 in

18)

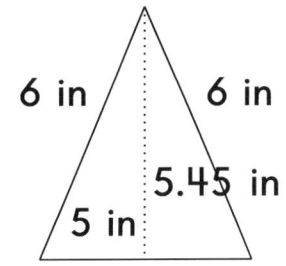

6 in   6 in
5.45 in
5 in

19)

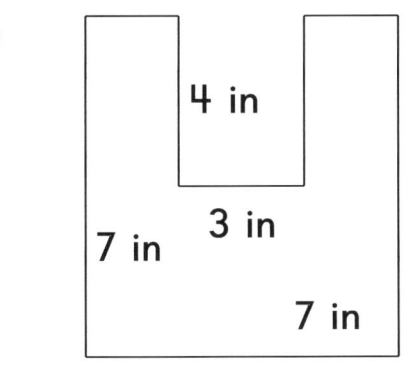

4 in
7 in   3 in
7 in

20)

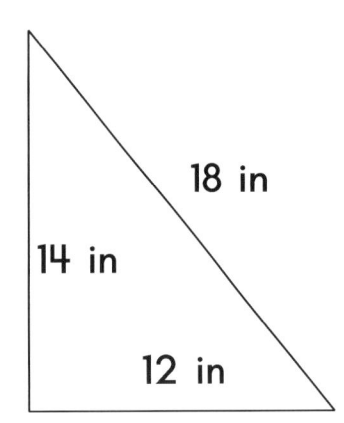

18 in
14 in
12 in

Math Workbook for Grade 7-8 Date: ____/____/_____

21)

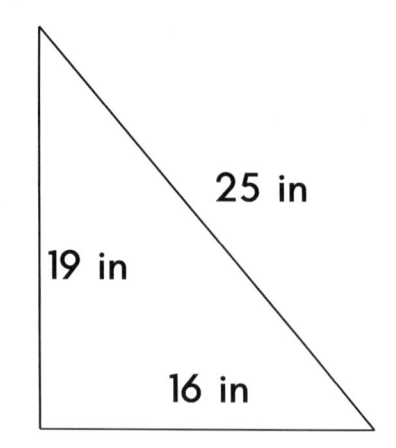

25 in
19 in
16 in

22)

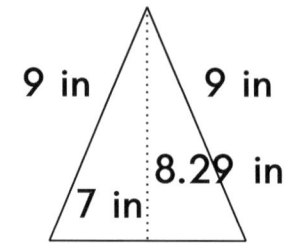

9 in   9 in
7 in 8.29 in

23)

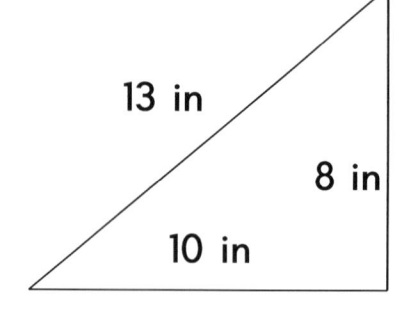

13 in
8 in
10 in

24)

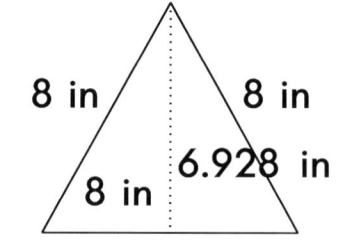

8 in   8 in
8 in 6.928 in

Math Workbook for Grade 7-8   Date: ____/____/_____

25) 8 in, 8 in, 7.42 in, 6 in

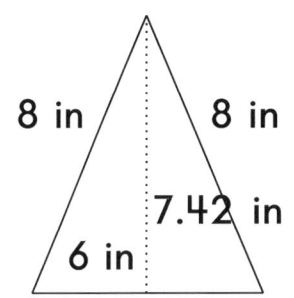

26) 6 in, 2 in, 7 in, 4 in

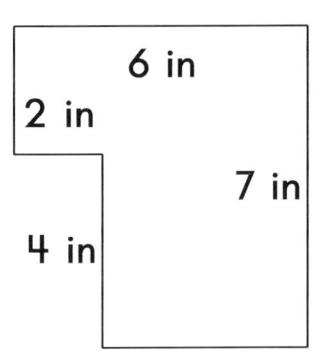

27) 9 in, 6 in, 6 in

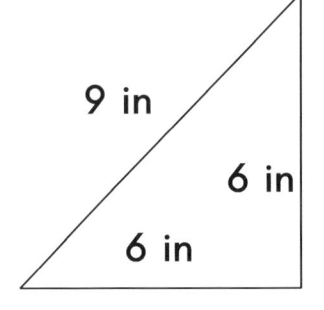

28) 8 in, 8 in, 7.42 in, 6 in

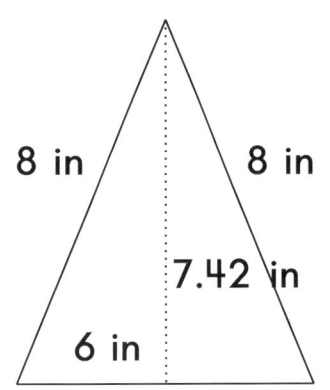

Math Workbook for Grade 7-8 Date: ____/____/_____

29)
- 15 in
- 12 in
- 10 in

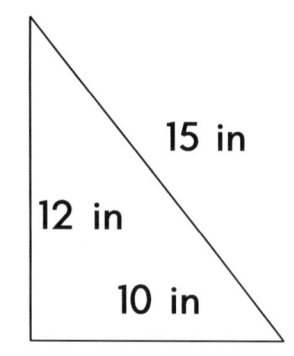

30)
- 10 in
- 8 in

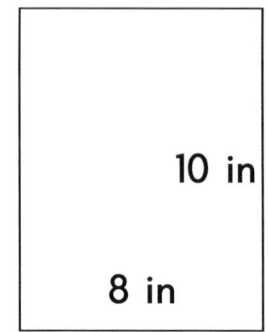

31)
- 8 in
- 8 in
- 7.85 in
- 4 in

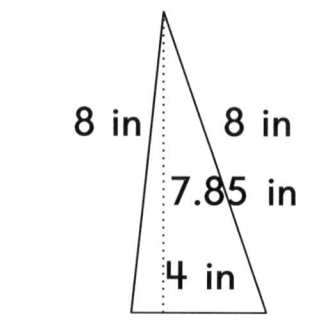

32)
- 6 in
- 4 in
- 6 in
- 3 in

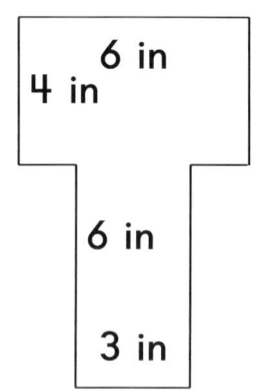

Math Workbook for Grade 7-8   Date: ____/____/_____

33)

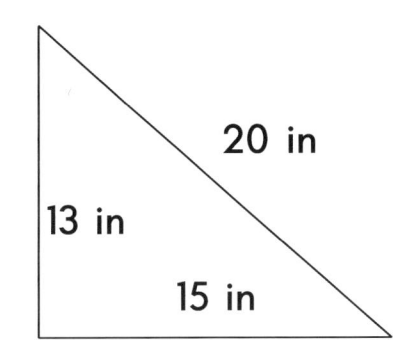

20 in
13 in
15 in

34)

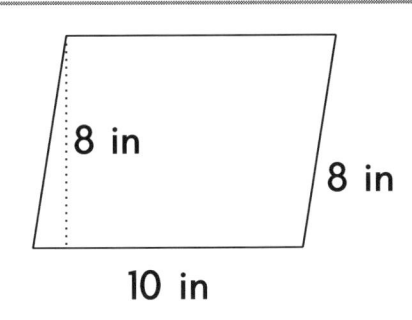

8 in
8 in
10 in

35)

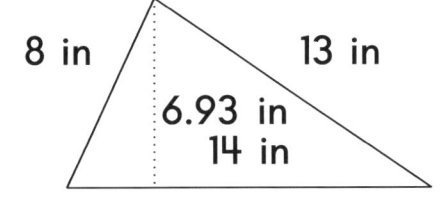

8 in
13 in
6.93 in
14 in

36)

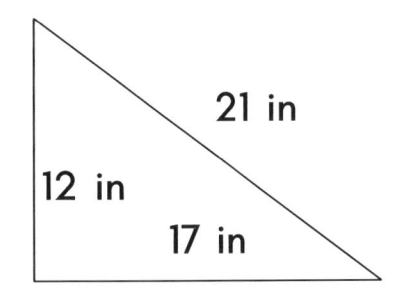

21 in
12 in
17 in

Math Workbook for Grade 7-8   Date: ____/____/_____

37)

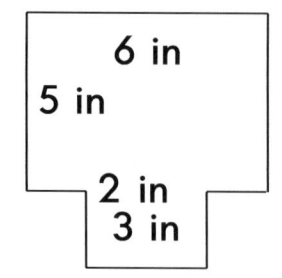

6 in
5 in
2 in
3 in

38)

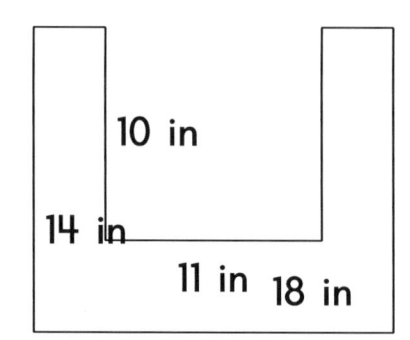

10 in
14 in
11 in   18 in

39)

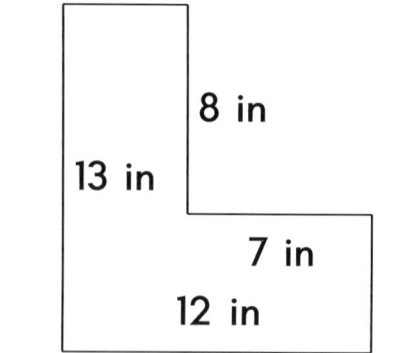

8 in
13 in
7 in
12 in

40)

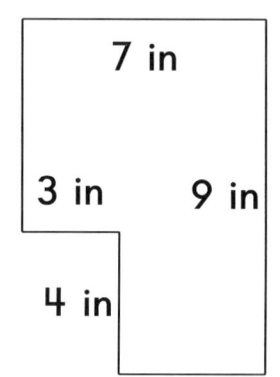

7 in
3 in   9 in
4 in

Pythagorean Theorem

The Pythagorean Theorem is a fundamental principle in geometry that relates the lengths of the sides of a right triangle. It states that in any right triangle, the square of the length of the hypotenuse (the side opposite the right angle) is equal to the sum of the squares of the lengths of the other two sides.

$$a^2 + b^2 = c^2$$

Let's use the Pythagorean Theorem to find the length of the hypotenuse (c) when $a=44$ and $b=78$.

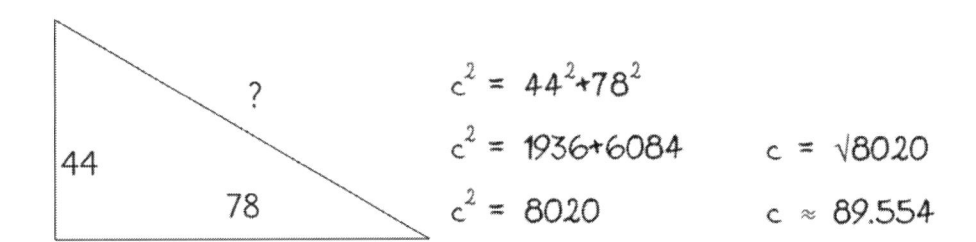

$c^2 = 44^2 + 78^2$

$c^2 = 1936 + 6084$

$c^2 = 8020$

$c = \sqrt{8020}$

$c \approx 89.554$

Anna School Learning

Math Workbook for Grade 7-8   Date: ____/____/_____

Pythagorean Theorem
Find the length of the side.

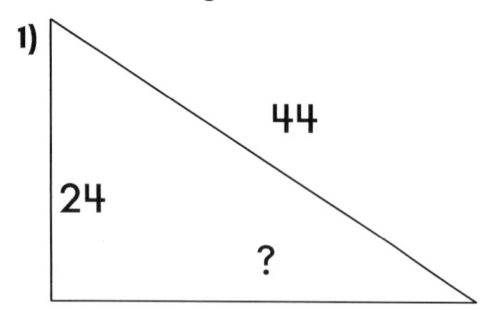

1) 44, 24, ?

2) 29, 12, ?

3) 81, 38, ?

4) 49, 22, ?

Math Workbook for Grade 7-8 Date: ____/____/_____

5)

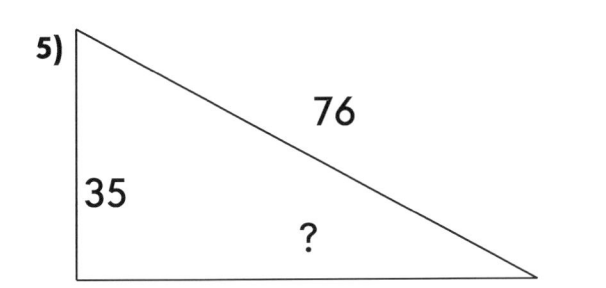

76
35
?

_____

6)

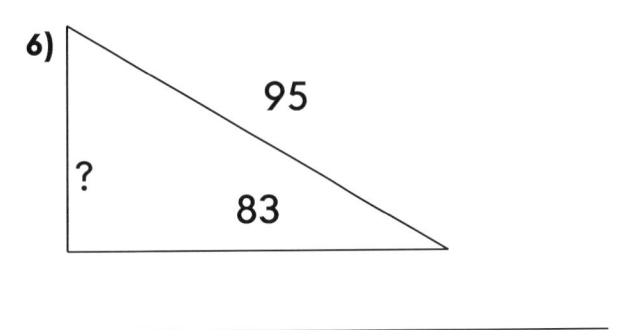

95
?
83

_____

7)

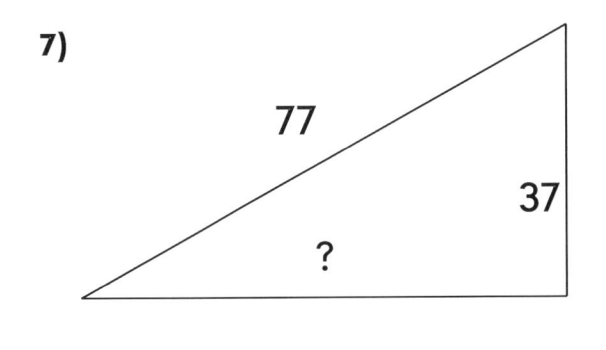

77
37
?

_____

8)

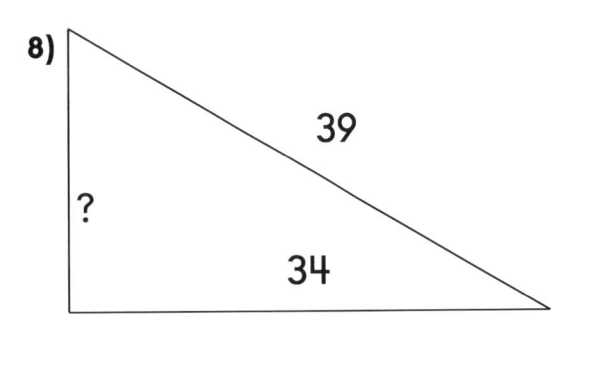

39
?
34

_____

65   Anna School Learning

Math Workbook for Grade 7-8   Date: ___/___/_____

9) 60, 31, ?

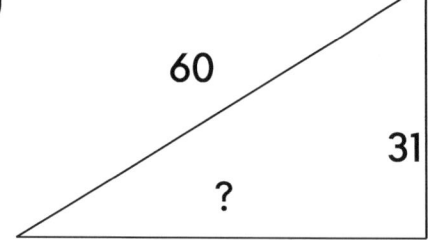

10) 128, ?, 113

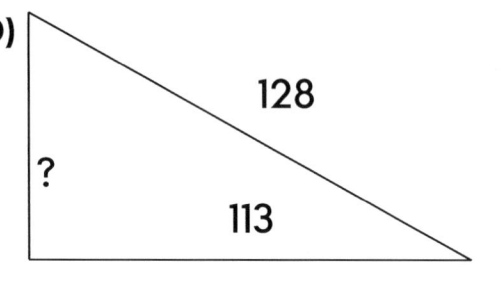

11) ?, 117, 55

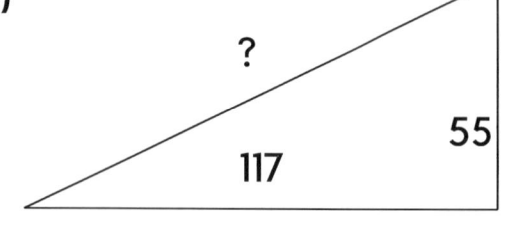

12) 56, ?, 50

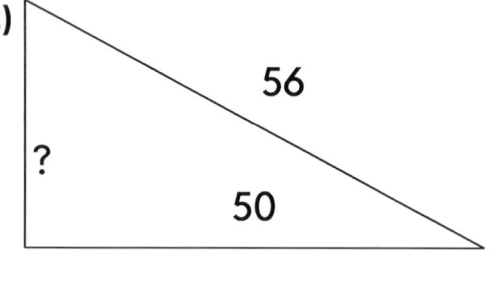

Math Workbook for Grade 7-8   Date: ___/___/_____

13)
38, 34, ?

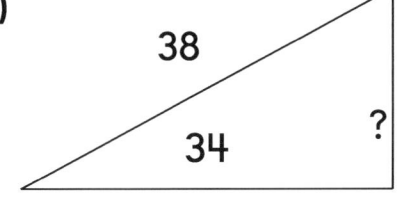

14)
54, ?, 126

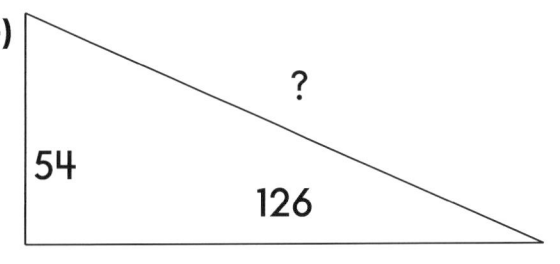

15)
?, 95, 176

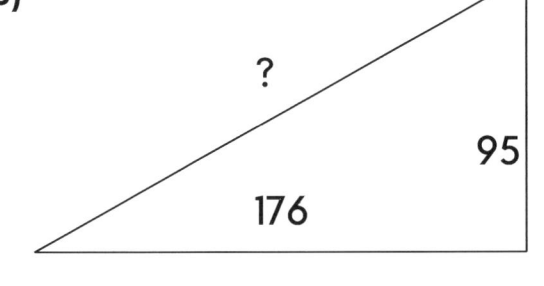

16)
203, 78, ?

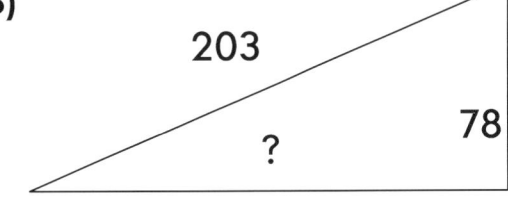

Math Workbook for Grade 7-8   Date: ____/____/_____

17) 46, ?, 90

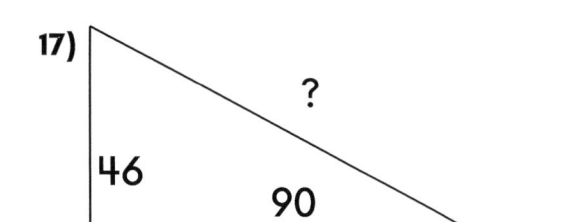

18) 115, 62, ?

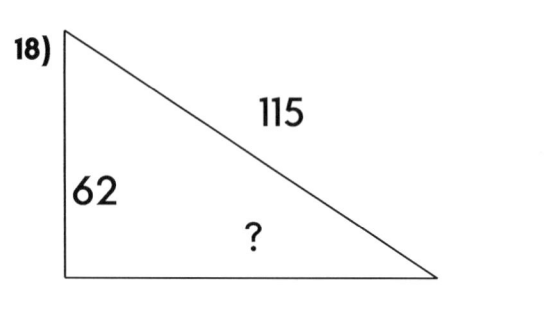

19) 187, 104, ?

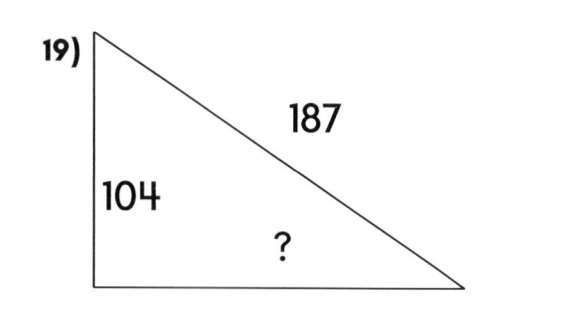

20) 118, 56, ?

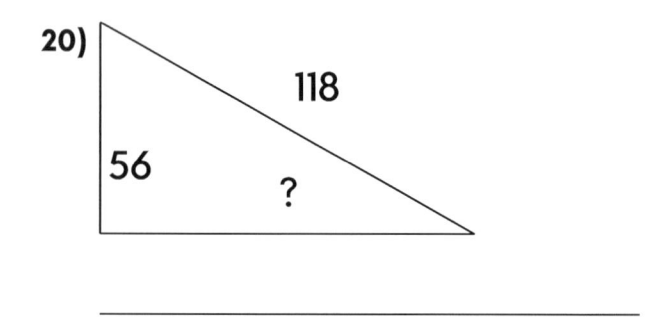

Math Workbook for Grade 7-8   Date: ____/____/_____

21) ? , 80, 74

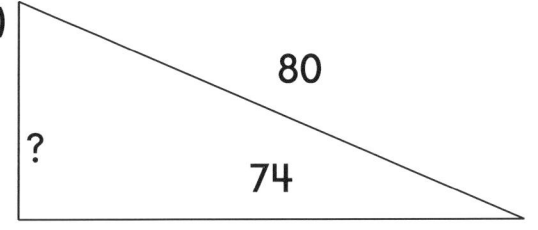

22) 157, ?, 65

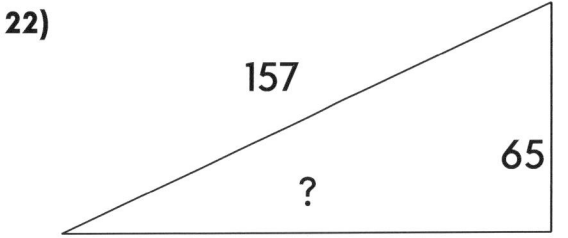

23) 12, ?, 31

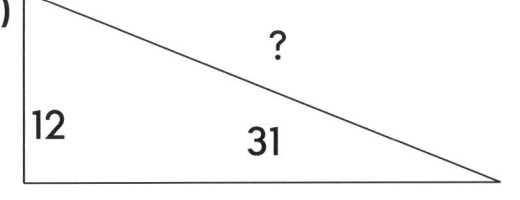

24) 28, ?, 56

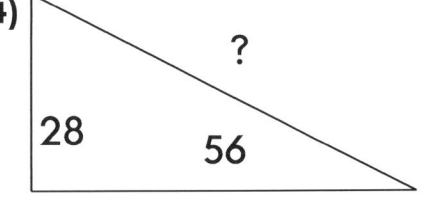

Volume and surface Area

Volume refers to the amount of space occupied by a three-dimensional object. For shapes like cubes or rectangular prisms, we calculate volume by multiplying their length, width, and height.

To find the volume V of a rectangular prism, we use the formula:

$$Volume = length \times width \times height$$

Surface Area represents the total area covering all the faces of a three-dimensional object. For shapes like cubes or rectangular prisms, we find the surface area by summing the areas of all its faces.

The formula for surface area SA of a cube or rectangular prism is:

$$Surface\ Area = 2lw + 2lh + 2wh$$

Where: l is the length, w is the width, and h is the height of the object.

For example: Let's find the Volume and Surface Area of following rectangular prisms:

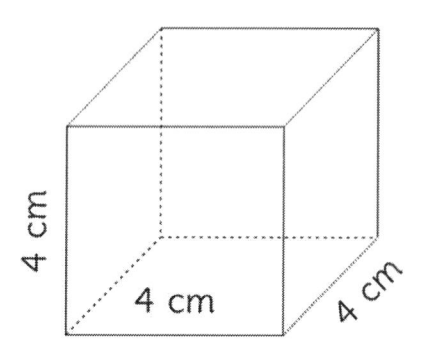

$$Volume = length \times width \times height$$
$$= 4 \times 4 \times 4$$
$$= 64\ cm^2$$

$$Surface\ Area = 2lw + 2lh + 2wh$$
$$= 2(4 \times 4) + 2(4 \times 4) + 2(4 \times 4)$$

Anna School Learning

$$= 32 + 32 + 32$$

$$= 96 \text{ cm}2$$

Different 3D objects have unique formulas for finding their volume and surface area. Here are some common ones:

1. **Cube:**
   - Volume: $V = s^3$ (where s is the length of one side of the cube)
   - Surface area: $SA = 6s^2$

2. **Sphere:**
   - Volume: $V = (\frac{4}{3})\pi r^3$ (where r is the radius of the sphere)
   - Surface area: $SA = 4\pi r^2$

3. **Cone:**
   - Volume: $V = (\frac{1}{3})\pi r^2 h$ (where r is the radius of the base and h is the height of the cone)
   - Surface area: $SA = \pi r^2 + \pi r \sqrt{(r^2 + h^2)}$

4. **Cylinder:**
   - Volume: $V = \pi r^2 h$ (where r is the radius of the base and h is the height of the cylinder)
   - Surface area: $SA = 2\pi r^2 + 2\pi r h$

5. **Pyramid:**
   - Volume: $V = (\frac{1}{3})Bh$ (where B is the area of the base and h is the height of the pyramid)
   - Surface area: $SA = B + \frac{1}{2}Pl$ (where P is the perimeter of the base and l is the slant height of the pyramid)

Anna School Learning

Math Workbook for Grade 7-8   Date: ____/____/_____

Volume and Surface Area

1) 8 ft, 6 ft

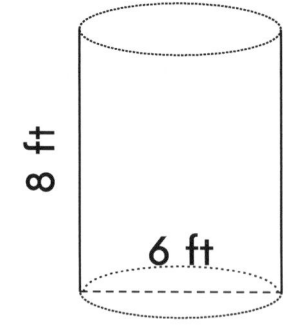

2) 4 ft, 8 ft

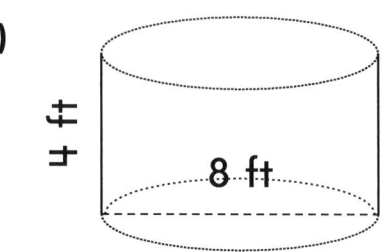

3) 4 ft

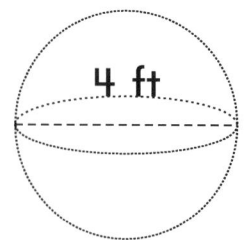

4) 8 cm, 6 cm, 11 cm

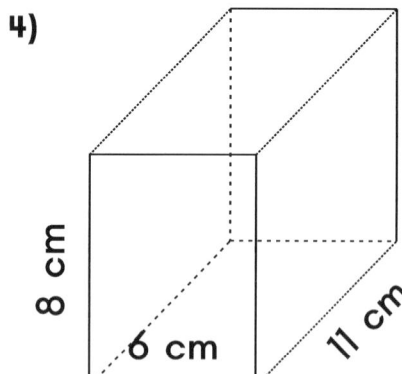

Math Workbook for Grade 7-8   Date: ____/____/_____

5)
10 cm 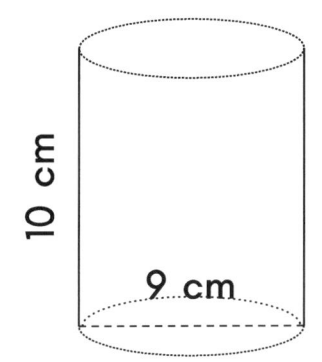
9 cm

6)
2 cm 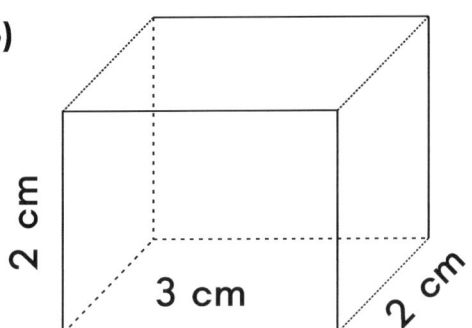
3 cm
2 cm

7)
2 ft 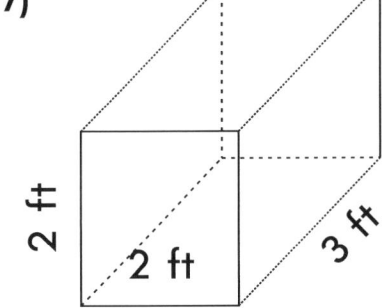
2 ft
3 ft

8)
6 ft 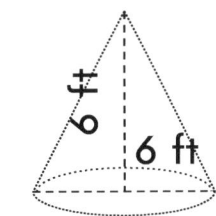
6 ft

Math Workbook for Grade 7-8   Date: ____/____/_____

9) 7 in

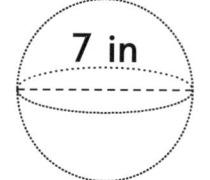

10) 6 cm, 7 cm

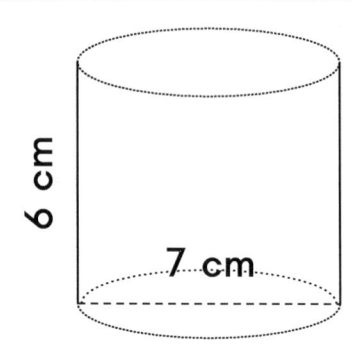

11) 9 ft, 5 ft, 8 ft

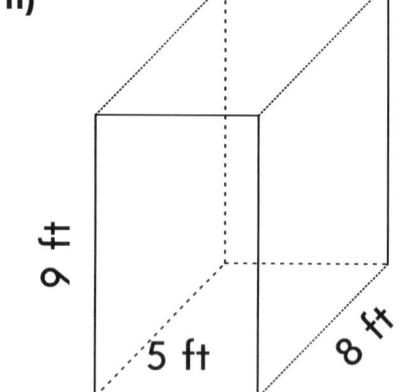

12) 3 cm, 3 cm, 3 cm

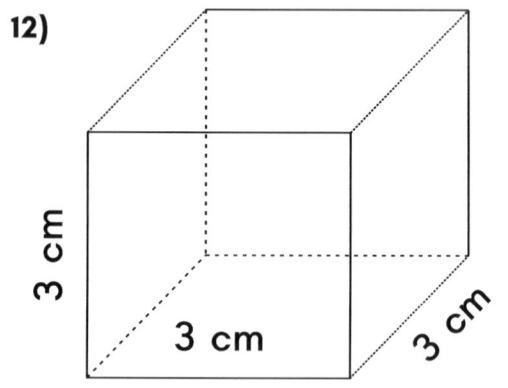

Math Workbook for Grade 7-8   Date: ____/____/_____

13) 7 in, 10 in, 9 in

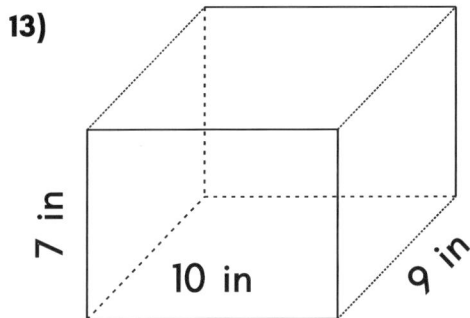

14) 2 ft, 4 ft

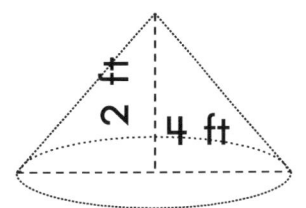

15) 4 cm, 3 cm

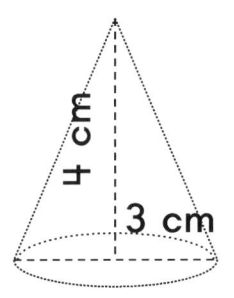

16) 9 ft, 6 ft

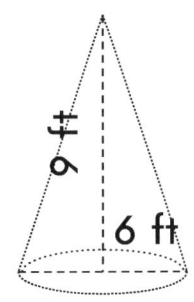

Math Workbook for Grade 7-8 Date: ____/____/_____

17) 8 cm, 9 cm, 10 cm

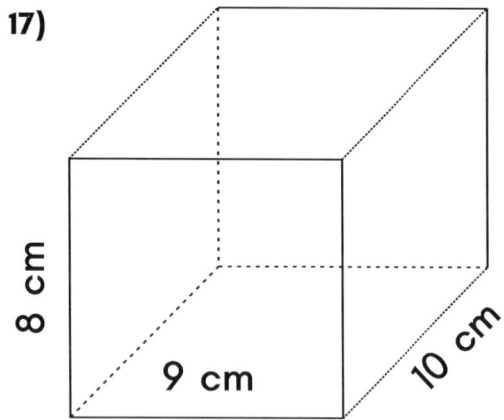

18) 6 in, 8 in

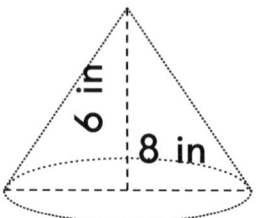

19) 6 cm, 3 cm

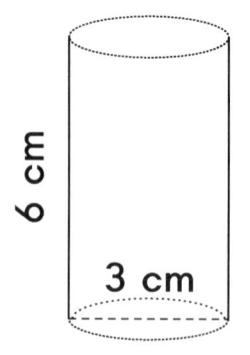

20) 6 ft, 8 ft, 5 ft

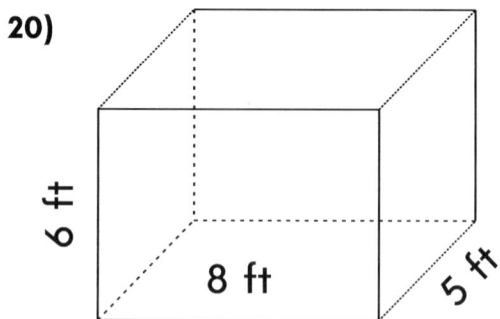

Math Workbook for Grade 7-8 Date: ____/____/_____

21) cone: 5 in (slant), 6 in (diameter)

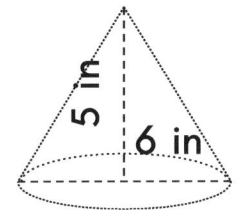

22) rectangular prism: 5 ft, 6 ft, 5 ft

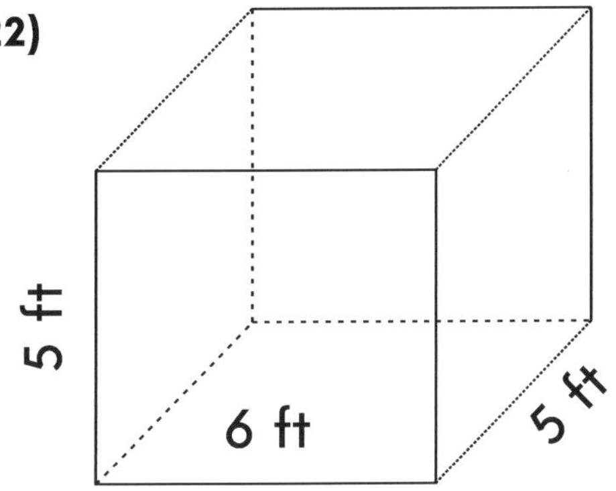

23) cylinder: 7 ft (height), 9 ft (diameter)

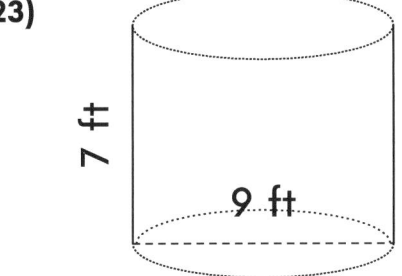

24) cube: 7 in, 7 in, 7 in

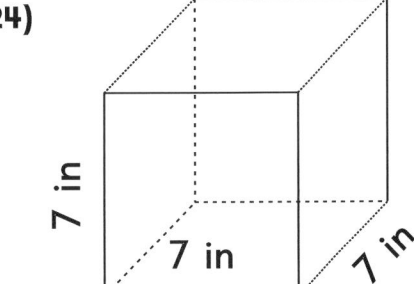

Math Workbook for Grade 7-8   Date: ____/____/_____

25)

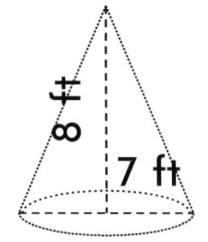

8 ft
7 ft

26)

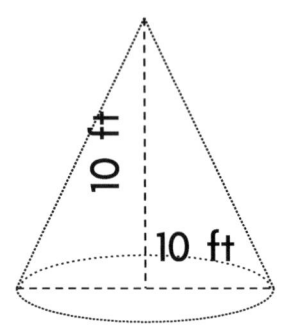

10 ft
10 ft

27)

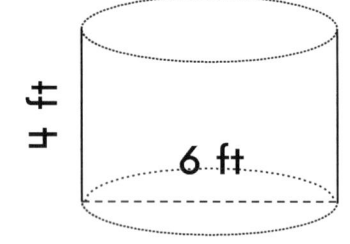

4 ft
6 ft

28)

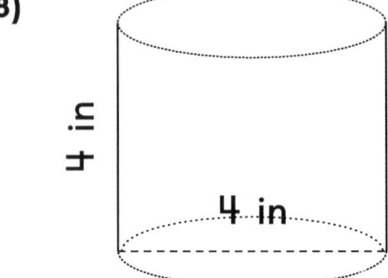

4 in
4 in

Math Workbook for Grade 7-8   Date: ____/____/_____

29)

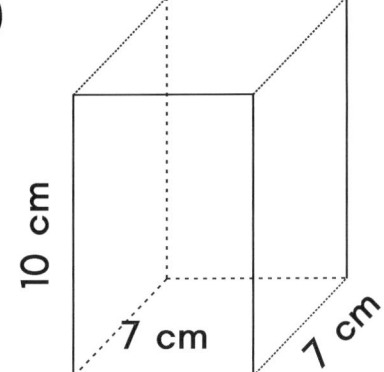

10 cm
7 cm
7 cm

30)

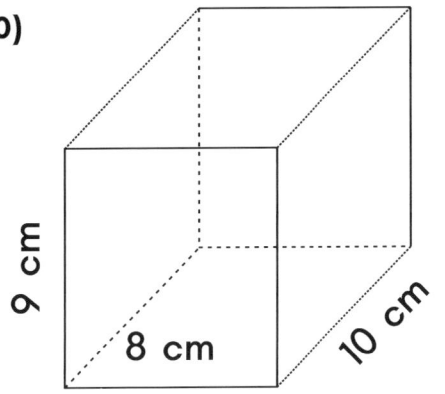

9 cm
8 cm
10 cm

31)

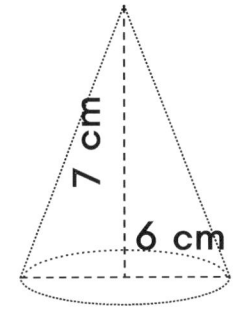

7 cm
6 cm

32)

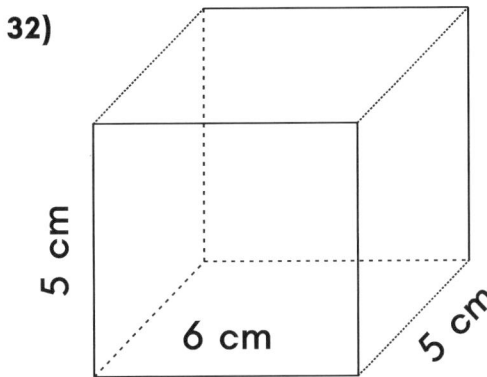

5 cm
6 cm
5 cm

Math Workbook for Grade 7-8

33) 7 ft, 6 ft, 8 ft

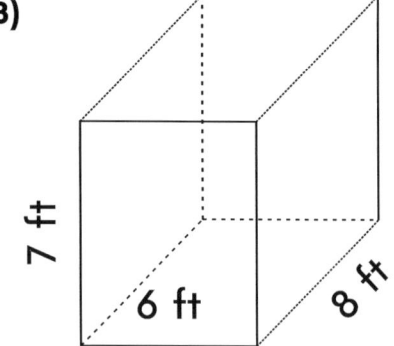

34) 7 cm, 8 cm

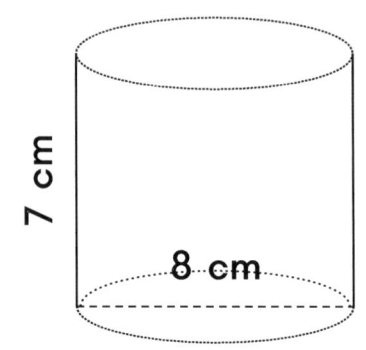

35) 10 ft, 9 ft, 9 ft

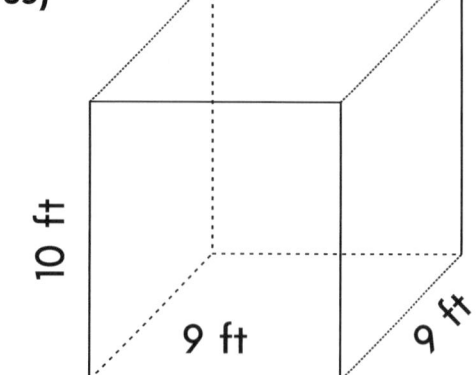

36) 4 in, 6 in, 4 in

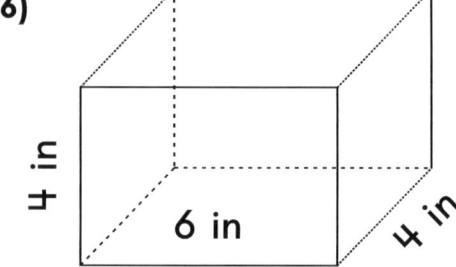

Math Workbook for Grade 7-8 Date: ____/____/_____

37) cone with 9 cm slant/height and 7 cm

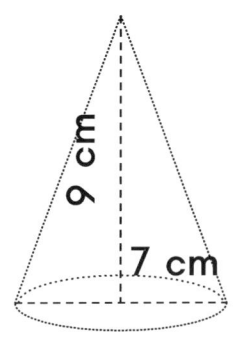

38) cone with 8 in and 8 in

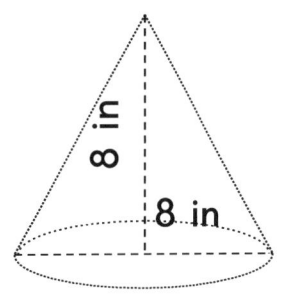

39) rectangular prism: 3 in, 2 in, 3 in

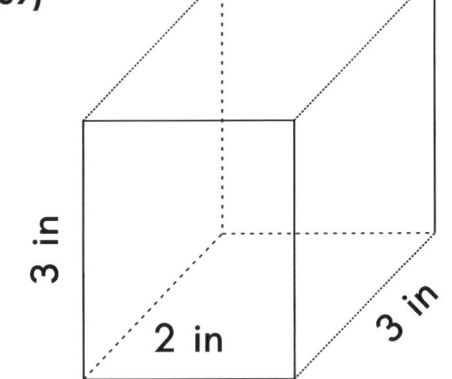

40) rectangular prism: 3 in, 4 in, 4 in

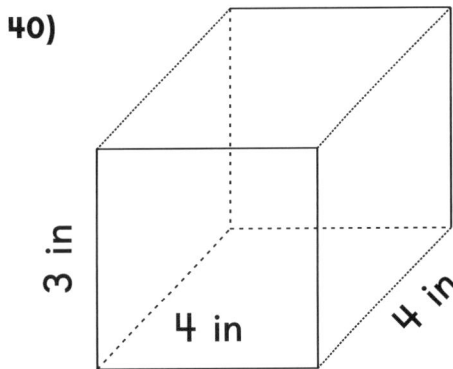

Statistics

Mean

The mean, also known as the average, is a measure of central tendency. To find the mean of a set of numbers:
- Add up all the numbers in the set.
- Divide the sum by the total count of numbers in the set.

For example: consider the set of numbers: 70, 72, 49, 69, 27, 76.

$$\text{Mean} = \frac{70 + 72 + 49 + 69 + 27 + 76}{6} = \frac{363}{6} = 60.5$$

Median

The median is a measure of central tendency that represents the middle value of a dataset when the values are arranged in ascending or descending order.

To find the median of a set of numbers:
- Arrange the numbers in ascending or descending order.
- If the total count of numbers is odd, the median is the middle value.
- If the total count of numbers is even, the median is the average of the two middle values.

For example: consider the set of numbers: 70, 72, 49, 69, 27, 76.

27, 49, 69, 70, 72, 76

$$\text{Median} = \frac{69 + 70}{2} = \frac{139}{2} = 69.5$$

Anna School Learning

Mode

The mode in statistics refers to the value that appears most frequently in a given set of data.

Let's consider the following set of numbers:
$$\{2, 4, 4, 5, 6, 6, 6, 7, 8, 8\}$$
In this set, the number 6 appears three times, more than any other number. Therefore, the mode of this dataset is 6.

It's possible for a dataset to have more than one mode if two or more numbers appear with the same highest frequency. In such cases, the dataset is considered multimodal. If no number repeats, the dataset is considered to have no mode.

For example:
$$\{2, 4, 4, 4, 5, 6, 6, 6, 7, 8, 8\}$$
In this date set, 4 and 6 appear three times. Therefore, this dataset is multimodal.

Range

In statistics, the range refers to the difference between the largest and smallest values in a dataset. It represents the spread or variability of the data.

For example, consider the dataset { 68, 13, 30, 18, 45, 76, 11}:

To calculate the range:
1. Arrange the data points in ascending order.
$$11, 13, 18, 30, 45, 68, 76$$
2. Subtract the smallest value from the largest value.
- The smallest value is 11.
- The largest value is 76.

   Range = Largest value - smallest value = 76 - 11 = 65.

Anna School Learning

Math Workbook for Grade 7-8 Date: ____/____/_____

Mean, Median, Mode, and Range

Find the Mean, Median, Mode and Range of the following sets of data.

1) 60, 81, 8, 61, 2, 66, 88
   Mean = _____   Median = _____
   Mode = _____   Range = _____

2) 33, 15, 99, 79, 37, 90
   Mean = _____   Median = _____
   Mode = _____   Range = _____

3) 26, 69, 14, 17, 79, 63, 48
   Mean = _____   Median = _____
   Mode = _____   Range = _____

4) 34, 5, 38, 56, 87, 70
   Mean = _____   Median = _____
   Mode = _____   Range = _____

Math Workbook for Grade 7-8   Date: ____/____/_____

5) 83, 78, 91, 69, 28, 10
   Mean = _____   Median = ____
   Mode = _____   Range = ____

6) 9, 35, 27, 3, 83, 69
   Mean = _____   Median = ____
   Mode = _____   Range = ____

7) 9, 87, 20, 90, 16, 44, 10
   Mean = _____   Median = ____
   Mode = _____   Range = ____

8) 11, 24, 85, 83, 60, 47, 71
   Mean = _____   Median = ____
   Mode = _____   Range = ____

9) 16, 55, 76, 55, 44, 52
   Mean = _____   Median = ____
   Mode = _____   Range = ____

Math Workbook for Grade 7-8   Date: ____/____/_____

10) 74, 31, 82, 11, 41, 45

Mean = _____ Median = _____
Mode = _____ Range = _____

11) 71, 70, 28, 55, 98, 67, 30

Mean = _____ Median = _____
Mode = _____ Range = _____

12) 47, 70, 75, 28, 43, 88, 93

Mean = _____ Median = _____
Mode = _____ Range = _____

13) 46, 76, 46, 98, 94, 32

Mean = _____ Median = _____
Mode = _____ Range = _____

14) 23, 56, 93, 54, 59, 72

Mean = _____ Median = _____
Mode = _____ Range = _____

Math Workbook for Grade 7-8   Date: ____/____/_____

15) 58, 32, 95, 77, 6, 10
    Mean = _____   Median = ____
    Mode = _____   Range = ____

16) 50, 71, 73, 40, 82, 69
    Mean = _____   Median = ____
    Mode = _____   Range = ____

17) 86, 17, 31, 99, 2, 41, 27
    Mean = _____   Median = ____
    Mode = _____   Range = ____

18) 33, 66, 50, 6, 97, 84
    Mean = _____   Median = ____
    Mode = _____   Range = ____

19) 83, 16, 9, 23, 16, 76
    Mean = _____   Median = ____
    Mode = _____   Range = ____

Math Workbook for Grade 7-8   Date: ____/____/_____

20) 74, 95, 27, 9, 98, 51
    Mean = _____   Median = _____
    Mode = _____   Range = _____

21) 92, 70, 19, 93, 18, 21, 7
    Mean = _____   Median = _____
    Mode = _____   Range = _____

22) 94, 77, 12, 77, 1, 23, 55
    Mean = _____   Median = _____
    Mode = _____   Range = _____

23) 53, 27, 27, 6, 9, 26
    Mean = _____   Median = _____
    Mode = _____   Range = _____

24) 98, 93, 22, 93, 41, 49
    Mean = _____   Median = _____
    Mode = _____   Range = _____

Anna School Learning

Math Workbook for Grade 7-8

ANSWERS

Page 1: Percentage
1. 4.8 2. 600 3. 600 4. 270 5. 500 6. 400 7. 1800
8. 240 9. 5% 10. 6 11. 2% 12. 27 13. 35% 14. 100
15. 80% 16. 75% 17. 14 18. 28 19. 10% 20. 200% 21. 100%
22. 600 23. 15% 24. 100 25. 10 26. 420 27. 90% 28. 600
29. 50% 30. 16

Page 3:
1. 33.864 2. 928 3. 6 4. 22.4% 5. 0.156 6. 28
7. 393 8. 28 9. 126.294 10. 7.2% 11. 2.3% 12. 36.7%
13. 2.376 14. 0.972 15. 43 16. 10.8% 17. 0.96 18. 0.6%
19. 0.4% 20. 0.1%

Page 5: Word Problems: Percent
1. 4 2. 39 3. 95 4. $120.00 5. 21 6. 1
7. $21.00 8. 23 9. $84.00 10. $91.00 11. 117 12. 126
13. 2 14. $10.00 15. 29 16. 4 17. $90.00 18. 33
19. 39 20. 58 21. $42.00 22. 2 23. 49 24. $151.00
25. $4.00 26. $3.00 27. 29 28. 4 29. $3.00 30. 54

Page 11: Ratio and Proportion Word Problems
1. 12.6 2. 19.33 3. 884.25 4. 288 5. 24.88 6. 16
7. 8 8. 7 9. 11.75 10. 16 11. 11.86 12. 2.5
13. 15.2 14. 667.33 15. 25.41 16. 18.12 17. 25.83 18. 669
19. 7.33 20. 691.2 21. 4.2 22. 6.44 23. 7.73 24. 11.97
25. 11.43 26. 8.57 27. 16 28. 858 29. 1,492.5 30. 34

Anna School Learning

Math Workbook for Grade 7-8

Page 21: Ratio Conversions

1.

	Ratio	Fraction	Percent	Decimal
a.	3:19	3/19	15.8%	0.158
b.	3:6	3/6	50%	0.5
c.	6:11	6/11	54.5%	0.545
d.	1:1	1/1	100%	1
e.	3:8	3/8	37.5%	0.375
f.	4:6	4/6	66.7%	0.667
g.	6:7	6/7	85.7%	0.857
h.	5:7	5/7	71.4%	0.714
i.	10:14	10/14	71.4%	0.714
j.	10:19	10/19	52.6%	0.526
k.	1:13	1/13	7.7%	0.077
l.	2:7	2/7	28.6%	0.286
m.	16:17	16/17	94.1%	0.941
n.	7:18	7/18	38.9%	0.389
o.	1:3	1/3	33.3%	0.333

2.

	Ratio	Fraction	Percent	Decimal
a.	9:12	9/12	75%	0.75
b.	8:17	8/17	47.1%	0.471
c.	3:5	3/5	60%	0.6
d.	16:19	16/19	84.2%	0.842
e.	6:20	6/20	30%	0.3
f.	20:20	20/20	100%	1
g.	1:4	1/4	25%	0.25
h.	2:5	2/5	40%	0.4
i.	6:11	6/11	54.5%	0.545
j.	7:15	7/15	46.7%	0.467
k.	3:11	3/11	27.3%	0.273
l.	2:14	2/14	14.3%	0.143
m.	1:16	1/16	6.2%	0.062
n.	9:15	9/15	60%	0.6
o.	16:17	16/17	94.1%	0.941

3.

	Ratio	Fraction	Percent	Decimal
a.	12:13	12/13	92.3%	0.923
b.	14:16	14/16	87.5%	0.875
c.	10:14	10/14	71.4%	0.714
d.	8:11	8/11	72.7%	0.727
e.	6:17	6/17	35.3%	0.353
f.	17:20	17/20	85%	0.85
g.	18:19	18/19	94.7%	0.947
h.	3:3	3/3	100%	1
i.	1:17	1/17	5.9%	0.059
j.	9:20	9/20	45%	0.45
k.	17:18	17/18	94.4%	0.944
l.	6:9	6/9	66.7%	0.667
m.	1:2	1/2	50%	0.5
n.	1:4	1/4	25%	0.25
o.	5:7	5/7	71.4%	0.714

Page 24: Order of Operations (PEMDAS)

1. 12　　**2.** 8　　**3.** 44　　**4.** 450　　**5.** 66　　**6.** 143　　**7.** 210

8. 17　　**9.** 910　　**10.** 30　　**11.** 1,032　　**12.** 19　　**13.** 292　　**14.** 333

15. 108　　**16.** 108　　**17.** 2.8　　**18.** 6,402　　**19.** −10　　**20.** 195　　**21.** 6

22. 1,609　　**23.** 14　　**24.** 36　　**25.** 2,923　　**26.** 0.9　　**27.** 121　　**28.** 102

29. 11　　**30.** 313

Page 27: Evaluate Expressions

1. 1 or 4　　**2.** 1　　**3.** 1　　**4.** 6　　**5.** 1　　**6.** 6

7. 4　　**8.** 1　　**9.** 3　　**10.** 1　　**11.** 9　　**12.** 1 or −6

13. 6　　**14.** 1　　**15.** 5　　**16.** 1　　**17.** 1　　**18.** 4 or −5

19. 9　　**20.** 9　　**21.** 8　　**22.** 1 or −1　　**23.** 1 or −5　　**24.** 3

25. 5 or −5　　**26.** 2　　**27.** 1　　**28.** 1　　**29.** 6　　**30.** 6

Page 31: Solving Inequalities

1. $b \leq 2$　　**2.** $m \geq -16$　　**3.** $b \geq 6/5$　　**4.** $x < -4$　　**5.** $y < -3$　　**6.** $k \geq -6$

7. $b > -1/2$　　**8.** $b > -3$　　**9.** $y \geq -14$　　**10.** $k \leq -1$　　**11.** $b > -4$　　**12.** $z > -13$

13. $z < -7$　　**14.** $k < 48$　　**15.** $m \leq -2$　　**16.** $m \leq -1$　　**17.** $b > -5/2$　　**18.** $y \leq 16$

19. $m < 13$　　**20.** $x \leq -21$

Page 36: Verbal Algebra

1. 9, 10, 11　　**2.** 6　　**3.** 4　　**4.** 6, 37　　**5.** 9

6. 18　　**7.** 48　　**8.** 4, 6, 8　　**9.** 9, 11　　**10.** 9

11. 4　　**12.** 6　　**13.** 3, 27　　**14.** 4, 6, 8, 10　　**15.** 3

Math Workbook for Grade 7-8

16. 5, 15 **17.** 4 **18.** 9 **19.** 3, 4, 5 **20.** 16

Page 40: Solving Equations: (One Side)

1. y = 6 **2.** y = 2 **3.** m = 42 **4.** m = 11 **5.** y = 12 **6.** k = 6 **7.** m = 6
8. k = 3 **9.** m = 22 **10.** k = 15 **11.** m = 14 **12.** y = 2 **13.** z = 8 **14.** k = 8
15. m = 5 **16.** z = 6 **17.** k = 126 **18.** y = 20 **19.** k = 6 **20.** m = 7 **21.** k = 20
22. z = 12 **23.** z = 18 **24.** k = 10 **25.** k = 16 **26.** m = 2 **27.** y = 12 **28.** z = 3
29. x = 10 **30.** z = 9

Page 43: Equations (Two Sides)

1. y = 9 **2.** y = 6 **3.** m = 4 **4.** z = 5 **5.** k = 3 **6.** x = 3 **7.** y = 2
8. z = 9 **9.** m = 2 **10.** m = 9 **11.** m = 7 **12.** k = 1 **13.** m = 9 **14.** y = 1
15. x = 7 **16.** x = 5 **17.** k = 8 **18.** x = 8 **19.** x = 2 **20.** z = 4 **21.** x = 7
22. m = 4 **23.** x = 7 **24.** y = 7 **25.** z = 5 **26.** y = 6 **27.** z = 5 **28.** k = 1
29. z = 4

Page 48: Cartesian Coordinates

1. 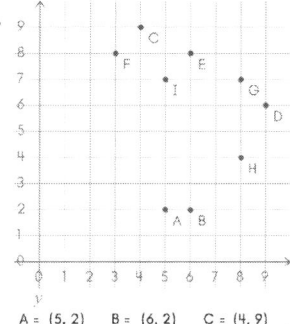
A = (5, 2)   B = (6, 2)   C = (4, 9)
D = (9, 6)   E = (6, 8)   F = (3, 8)
G = (8, 7)   H = (8, 4)   I = (5, 7)

2. 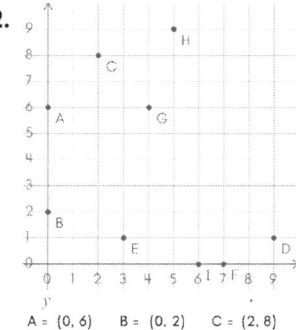
A = (0, 6)   B = (0, 2)   C = (2, 8)
D = (9, 1)   E = (3, 1)   F = (7, 0)
G = (4, 6)   H = (5, 9)   I = (6, 0)

3. 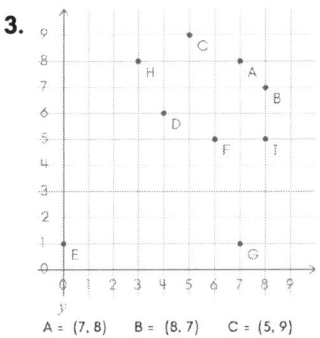
A = (7, 8)   B = (8, 7)   C = (5, 9)
D = (4, 6)   E = (0, 1)   F = (6, 5)
G = (7, 1)   H = (3, 8)   I = (8, 5)

Anna School Learning

Math Workbook for Grade 7-8

Page 51: Cartesian Coordinates With Four Quadrants

1. 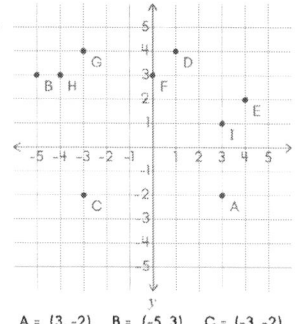
A = (3, -2)   B = (-5, 3)   C = (-3, -2)
D = (1, 4)   E = (4, 2)   F = (0, 3)
G = (-3, 4)   H = (-4, 3)   I = (3, 1)

2. 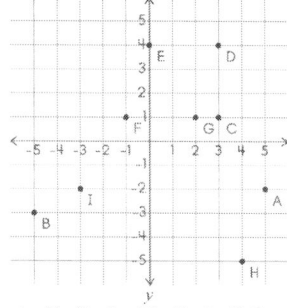
A = (5, -2)   B = (-5, -3) C = (3, 1)
D = (3, 4)   E = (0, 4)   F = (-1, 1)
G = (2, 1)   H = (4, -5)   I = (-3, -2)

3. 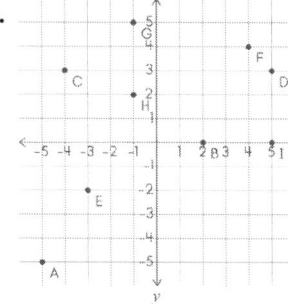
A = (-5, -5) B = (2, 0)   C = (-4, 3)
D = (5, 3)   E = (-3, -2) F = (4, 4)
G = (-1, 5)   H = (-1, 2)   I = (5, 0)

Page 54: Area and Perimeter

1. P=42 A=80
2. P=48 A=108.43
3. P=48 A=96
4. P=54 A=182
5. P=33 A=45
6. P=32 A=45
7. P=33 A=52.39
8. P=46 A=94
9. P=33 A=44
10. P=28 A=48
11. P=54 A=119
12. P=32 A=63
13. P=28 A=27.15
14. P=37 A=60.5
15. P=26 A=35
16. P=24 A=24.5
17. P=50 A=90
18. P=17 A=13.62
19. P=36 A=37
20. P=44 A=84
21. P=60 A=152
22. P=25 A=29.02
23. P=31 A=40
24. P=24 A=27.71
25. P=22 A=22.26
26. P=26 A=34
27. P=21 A=18
28. P=22 A=22.26
29. P=37 A=60
30. P=36 A=80
31. P=20 A=15.7
32. P=32 A=42
33. P=48 A=97.5
34. P=36 A=80
35. P=35 A=48.51
36. P=50 A=102
37. P=26 A=36
38. P=84 A=142
39. P=50 A=100
40. P=32 A=51

Page 64: Pythagorean Theorem

1. S=36.878
2. S=26.401
3. S=71.533
4. S=43.784
5. S=67.461
6. S=46.217
7. S=67.528
8. S=19.105
9. S=51.371
10. S=60.125
11. S=129.283
12. S=25.219
13. S=16.971
14. S=137.084
15. S=200.002
16. S=187.417
17. S=101.074
18. S=96.856
19. S=155.412
20. S=103.865
21. S=30.397
22. S=142.913
23. S=33.242
24. S=62.610

Page 70: Volume and Surface Area

1. V=226.19 ft³ ft³   SA=207 ft² ft²
2. V=201.06 ft³ ft³   SA=201 ft² ft²

Anna School Learning

Math Workbook for Grade 7-8

3. V=34 ft³ ft³ SA=50 ft² ft²
4. V=528 cm³ cm³ SA=404 cm² cm²
5. V=636.17 cm³ cm³ SA=410 cm² cm²
6. V=12 cm³ cm³ SA=32 cm² cm²
7. V=12 ft³ ft³ SA=32 ft² ft²
8. V=57 ft³ ft³ SA=91 ft² ft²
9. V=180 in³ in³ SA=154 in² in²
10. V=230.91 cm³ cm³ SA=209 cm² cm²
11. V=360 ft³ ft³ SA=314 ft² ft²
12. V=27 cm³ cm³ SA=54 cm² cm²
13. V=630 in³ in³ SA=446 in² in²
14. V=8 ft³ ft³ SA=30 ft² ft²
15. V=9 cm³ cm³ SA=27 cm² cm²
16. V=85 ft³ ft³ SA=118 ft² ft²
17. V=720 cm³ cm³ SA=484 cm² cm²
18. V=101 in³ in³ SA=141 in² in²
19. V=42.41 cm³ cm³ SA=71 cm² cm²
20. V=240 ft³ ft³ SA=236 ft² ft²
21. V=47 in³ in³ SA=83 in² in²
22. V=150 ft³ ft³ SA=170 ft² ft²
23. V=445.32 ft³ ft³ SA=325 ft² ft²
24. V=343 in³ in³ SA=294 in² in²
25. V=103 ft³ ft³ SA=134 ft² ft²
26. V=262 ft³ ft³ SA=254 ft² ft²
27. V=113.10 ft³ ft³ SA=132 ft² ft²
28. V=50.27 in³ in³ SA=75 in² in²
29. V=490 cm³ cm³ SA=378 cm² cm²
30. V=720 cm³ cm³ SA=484 cm² cm²
31. V=66 cm³ cm³ SA=100 cm² cm²
32. V=150 cm³ cm³ SA=170 cm² cm²
33. V=336 ft³ ft³ SA=292 ft² ft²
34. V=351.86 cm³ cm³ SA=276 cm² cm²
35. V=810 ft³ ft³ SA=522 ft² ft²
36. V=96 in³ in³ SA=128 in² in²
37. V=115 cm³ cm³ SA=145 cm² cm²
38. V=134 in³ in³ SA=163 in² in²
39. V=18 in³ in³ SA=42 in² in²
40. V=48 in³ in³ SA=80 in² in²

Page 80: Mean, Median, Mode, and Range

1. Mean = 52.286, Median = 61, Mode = none, Range = 86
2. Mean = 58.833, Median = 58, Mode = none, Range = 84
3. Mean = 45.143, Median = 48, Mode = none, Range = 65
4. Mean = 48.333, Median = 47, Mode = none, Range = 82
5. Mean = 59.833, Median = 73.5, Mode = none, Range = 81
6. Mean = 37.667, Median = 31, Mode = none, Range = 80
7. Mean = 39.429, Median = 20, Mode = none, Range = 81

Math Workbook for Grade 7-8

8. Mean = 54.429, Median = 60, Mode = none, Range = 74
9. Mean = 49.667, Median = 53.5, Mode = 55, Range = 60
10. Mean = 47.333, Median = 43, Mode = none, Range = 71
11. Mean = 59.857, Median = 67, Mode = none, Range = 70
12. Mean = 63.429, Median = 70, Mode = none, Range = 65
13. Mean = 65.333, Median = 61, Mode = 46, Range = 66
14. Mean = 59.5, Median = 57.5, Mode = none, Range = 70
15. Mean = 46.333, Median = 45, Mode = none, Range = 89
16. Mean = 64.167, Median = 70, Mode = none, Range = 42
17. Mean = 43.286, Median = 31, Mode = none, Range = 97
18. Mean = 56, Median = 58, Mode = none, Range = 91
19. Mean = 37.167, Median = 19.5, Mode = 16, Range = 74
20. Mean = 59, Median = 62.5, Mode = none, Range = 89
21. Mean = 45.714, Median = 21, Mode = none, Range = 86
22. Mean = 48.429, Median = 55, Mode = 77, Range = 93
23. Mean = 24.667, Median = 26.5, Mode = 27, Range = 47
24. Mean = 66, Median = 71, Mode = 93, Range = 76